TO
AND NOT
TO YIELD

How Advances in Information and Firepower
Can Transform Theater Warfare

David A. Ochmanek
Edward R. Harshberger
David E. Thaler
Glenn A. Kent

PREPARED FOR THE UNITED STATES AIR FORCE

Project Air Force
RAND

Approved for public release; distribution unlimited

The research reported here was sponsored by the United States Air Force under Contract F49642-96-C-0001. Further information may be obtained from the Strategic Planning Division, Directorate of Plans, Hq USAF.

Library of Congress Cataloging-in-Publication Data

To find, and not to yield : how advances in information and
   firepower can transform theater warfare / David Ochmanek ...
   [et al.].
         p.   cm.
      "Prepared for the United States Air Force by RAND's Project
   AIR FORCE."
      "MR-958-AF."
      ISBN 0-8330-2612-7 (alk. paper)
      1. Military planning—United States.   2. United States—Armed
   Forces—Operational readiness.   3. United States—Armed
   Forces—Weapons systems.   I. Ochmanek, David A.   II. United
   States. Air Force.   III. Project AIR FORCE. (U.S.).
   U153
   [.W56   1998]
   355.4 ' 0973—dc21   98-16852
                                                                      CIP

RAND is a nonprofit institution that helps improve policy and decisionmaking through research and analysis. RAND's publications do not necessarily reflect the opinions or policies of its research sponsors.

The cover illustration shows (clockwise from the top left) an AH-64 Apache helicopter, the F-15E Strike Eagle aircraft, and a missile launched from the Army Tactical Missile System (ATACMS). The background image is drawn from an E-8 Joint Surveillance and Target Attack Radar System (JSTARS) screen display. It depicts moving vehicles within a portion of the Kuwaiti theater of operations during the Iraqi retreat from Kuwait City in February 1991.

Published 1998 by RAND
1700 Main Street, P.O. Box 2138, Santa Monica, CA 90407-2138
1333 H St., N.W., Washington, D.C. 20005-4707
RAND URL: http://www.rand.org/
To order RAND documents or to obtain additional information,
contact Distribution Services: Telephone: (310) 451-7002;
Fax: (310) 451-6915; Internet: order@rand.org

Though much is taken, much abides; and though
We are not now that strength which in old days
Moved earth and heaven, that which we are, we are;
One equal temper of heroic hearts,
Made weak by time and fate, but strong in will
To strive, to seek, to find, and not to yield.

—Alfred Lord Tennyson, *Ulysses*

The Art of war is simple enough. Find out where your enemy is. Get at him as soon as you can. Strike at him as hard as you can and as often as you can, and keep moving on.

—Ulysses S. Grant

PREFACE

"We are surrounded by insurmountable opportunities."

—Pogo

Ironically perhaps, these are trying times for American defense planners. On the one hand, U.S. armed forces today are perhaps better prepared than ever before to protect the nation and to defend its interests around the globe. With the Cold War behind us, U.S. forces continue to enjoy a legacy of decades of investment in research and development, in modern weapons, and in extensive, realistic training. And by any measure, either in absolute terms or relative to the rest of the world, the United States is devoting a substantial level of resources to defense.

Yet it is difficult to avoid the sense that the nation is not focusing its defense resources as well as it could on meeting emerging threats and challenges. Over the past four years, modernization spending (as measured by the combination of Research, Development, Test, and Evaluation (RDT&E) and procurement funding) has been at its lowest level since 1977. Moreover, the share of spending on procurement—the expenditures that actually place new equipment into the hands of soldiers, sailors, and airmen—has fallen at a disproportionate rate. Procurement spending by the Department of Defense is now at its lowest level since the beginning of the Korean War.

More to the point, our potential adversaries may have profited more from the lessons of the Gulf War than our own defense establishment. There is ample evidence that the military forces of key regional powers are emphasizing improvements in such areas as ballistic and cruise missiles, weapons of mass destruction, modern air defenses, low-cost antiship weapons, and other capabilities that could be used to deter or impede U.S. forces' access to overseas theaters and to suppress their tempo of operations once deployed. It is not evident that U.S. operational concepts for deploying or employing forces are adjusting to these emerging challenges. Nor is there a consensus within the U.S. defense community to capitalize on unique and enduring U.S. advantages in rapidly deployable firepower and information systems, the early potential of which was demonstrated in Operation Desert Storm. Left unchecked, these trends could lead to a situation a decade hence in which U.S. forces, though sizable and well-trained, lack the capabilities they need to defeat aggression by a capable opponent without risking unacceptably high casualties and costs.

As is often the case, the problems stem not so much from technical barriers as from the difficulty in discerning that the risks of adopting new approaches to warfare are increasingly outweighed by the risks of holding onto more traditional approaches. New systems are emerging that can enable operational concepts well suited to meeting the demands of the future, but many of these programs are vulnerable to unnecessarily prolonged development schedules or even cancellation because of misguided funding priorities.

This report does not argue that the nation should be spending more on defense. It does argue that the Department of Defense should reexamine its force mix and investment priorities in order to exploit more fully and more rapidly important opportunities that exist to enhance U.S. capabilities for rapid power projection. The analysis set forth here should be useful to anyone with a serious interest in U.S. national security and defense planning, particularly those interested in capabilities needed to deter—and to prevail in—major theater conflicts.

PROJECT AIR FORCE

Project AIR FORCE, a division of RAND, is the Air Force's federally funded research and development center (FFRDC) for studies and analyses. It provides the Air Force with independent analyses of policy alternatives affecting the development, employment, combat readiness, and support of current and future air and space forces.

Research is performed in three programs: Strategy and Doctrine, Force Modernization and Employment, and Resource Management and System Acquisition.

CONTENTS

TABLES

The military forces of the United States are on the threshold of fielding new capabilities that, in concert, represent a revolutionary transformation in the ability to prosecute large-scale theater warfare. These capabilities, if fully exploited, can allow comparatively small numbers of forces to observe, assess, engage, and effectively attack enemy assets—especially moving land, sea, and air forces—over a large area. These new capabilities are thus well suited to meeting the needs of a demanding U.S. defense strategy that calls for forces that can rapidly project military power over long distances, apply that power in a discriminate fashion, and achieve highly asymmetric, favorable outcomes.

Despite the promise of these emerging capabilities, it is not clear that U.S. forces will be assured of prevailing over their adversaries in future major theater conflicts. Our potential enemies are not standing still—many already have lethal chemical and biological weapons and delivery vehicles, antiship mines and missiles, and capable air defenses, all of which can impede the deployment and employment of U.S. forces in hostile regions. Spreading technology and an open global arms market will allow nations with enough money and technical competence to field more-advanced versions of these weapons in the years to come. Thus, new challenges to U.S. power projection operations are arising.

But the most important factors determining the future balance between the capabilities of U.S. forces and those of our adversaries are in our own hands: The Department of Defense (DoD) may not be making the most of its considerable resources to develop and field with dispatch the new capabilities essential to defeating future threats. Overall U.S. force structure has been more or less frozen since the early 1990s. At the same time, the press of a heavy tempo of operations has placed considerable strain on many elements of U.S. active and reserve forces, imposing a steady drain on maintenance and training budgets. These realities have reinforced an innate and generally well-founded reluctance among U.S. force planners to trade force structure for qualitatively new capabilities. And despite determined efforts by DoD's leadership to downsize and modernize its huge support infrastructure, gaining meaningful savings from these accounts is proving to be a difficult and time-consuming task.

Hence, while the technical and operational communities within the U.S. defense establishment are generating impressive new opportunities for meeting emerging needs, these opportunities too often are postponed or abandoned because of inappropriate funding priorities. This is regrettable because traditional approaches to theater warfare, in which massed land forces with massive firepower are relied upon to defeat enemy ground forces, are not likely to be successful in the face of some important future challenges. Competent adversaries will seek to exploit surprise, speed of maneuver, and access denial capabilities to seize important objectives quickly before large-scale U.S. and allied defensive forces can be brought to bear. Without high-leverage enhancements that can allow forward-based and rapidly deploying forces to locate, identify, and destroy attacking forces, we may find it increasingly difficult to deter and defeat this kind of aggression.

Fortunately, new operational concepts are emerging that can address this endemic problem. For example, fixed-wing fighter and bomber aircraft, directed to their targets by theater surveillance and control systems and equipped with smart antiarmor munitions, can be an order of magnitude more effective in destroying mechanized ground forces than similar forces of the recent past. Similarly, these surveillance and control systems, along with advanced munitions, are making U.S. attack helicopters, long-range missiles, and artillery vastly more effective. Given sufficient shifts of investment toward these and other capabilities, it now appears possible to halt a large-scale combined arms offensive with forces that can be brought to bear within a matter of days rather than months.

There is much more to this new approach to power projection than just killing tanks, however. In regions where U.S. interests face threats of short-notice aggression, the key components of a modern U.S. "halt force" include:

- Joint forces deployed forward in peacetime that can monitor developments, train with allied and indigenous forces, and conduct initial defensive operations should deterrence fail

- Airlift, aerial refueling aircraft, and prepositioned assets for rapid deployment of reinforcements

- Forces that can protect rear area assets—such as airfields, logistic hubs, command centers, and ports—from air and missile attacks

- Forces that can quickly wrest from the enemy control of operations in the air, opening up enemy territory and forces to observation and attack from the air

- Airborne and space-based surveillance and control assets that can locate and characterize enemy maneuver forces and mobile air defenses in near-real time and pass that information to attack platforms

- Forces that can damage and destroy attacking enemy maneuver forces and their lines of communication, using munitions that offer a high probability of kill for each round expended, regardless of weather

- Small (brigade-sized) but highly capable maneuver forces able to defend key theater objectives against enemy ground forces that might survive or might avoid heavy attacks by longer range allied firepower assets.

Systems to provide these capabilities either exist today or are in advanced stages of development. If fielded in sufficient numbers, they would allow U.S. forces to halt armored invasions promptly, even under the stressing circumstances of a short-warning attack supported by concerted efforts to deny U.S. expeditionary forces access to the region of conflict. But investments in key elements of this halt capability are lagging: Under current plans, by 2005 U.S. inventories of advanced antiarmor munitions will be significantly smaller than those needed for two plausibly stressing major conflicts. Other programs at risk include high-leverage systems for theater surveil-lance and for sensor-to-shooter communications, avionics and other upgrades to existing aircraft to allow best use of advanced munitions, advanced concepts for suppressing modern surface-to-air missile (SAM) systems, and prepositioning of wartime assets in the Gulf region.

Given projections of a flat or declining DoD budget, investing ade-quately in these and other critical capabilities will require cuts in other accounts. Because it is so important that U.S. and allied forces prevail in the opening phase of a major conflict, if cuts must be im-posed upon deployable forces, they should, in general, come from systems and units that are not available for the halt phase; that is, from later-arriving forces intended for use in a counteroffensive. In our estimation, cuts of 10 to 15 percent in these forces would be sufficient to fund robust modernization of forces for two nearly si-multaneous halt operations.

Such cuts are warranted both because of the importance of the early halt of enemy forces and because advanced information and fire-power systems enable a shift in the division of labor on the battle-field. Heretofore, longer-range firepower systems, such as aircraft, missiles, and artillery, were seen primarily as *delaying and disrupting* attacking enemy ground forces, whereas heavy ground forces and supporting fires were relied upon to play the leading role in *destroy-ing and halting* the enemy. Henceforth, longer-range firepower will be increasingly relied upon to bear the greatest share of this burden. This shift represents a new approach to the conduct of joint theater campaigns that should prompt a thorough review of our operational concepts, force mix, and investment priorities.

ACKNOWLEDGMENTS

This report presents results from work by an interdisciplinary team assembled by RAND to assist staff at Headquarters, United States Air Force, during a series of DoD-wide reviews of future U.S. military capabilities. The work was sponsored by Major General Charles D. Link, who was Special Assistant to the Chief of Staff, National Defense Review. We are indebted to General Link and his staff, headed by Colonel David Deptula and, later, by Lieutenant Colonel Stephen McNamara, who played important roles in helping to conceptualize the research as it proceeded and in focusing it on issues of greatest concern to analysts and decisionmakers in the joint arena. Colonel Rusty O'Brien and his team in the Air Staff's Deep Attack Group were also intimately involved in helping shape our research, both as colleagues and in providing a window into ongoing joint studies.

The authors wish to thank a number of their colleagues at RAND—some members of the project team and some not—who contributed to the formulation and refinement of portions of this work. They include first and foremost Brent Bradley, who oversaw the project and provided careful guidance throughout, and Paul Davis, whose own work encompasses many of the areas addressed herein and who provided a thorough and thoughtful review of an early draft. Others at RAND who merit special mention are John Bordeaux and Daniel Norton, who contributed to the briefing based on the work documented in this report; Alex Hou, who reviewed many of our calculations; Bart Bennett, Brian Chow, Jeff Hagen, Steve Hosmer, Gary Lieberson, John Matsumura, and Donald Stevens, whose work has influenced ours in numerous ways; and Roger Brown, Carl

Builder, John Gordon, Richard Kugler, and Bruce Pirnie, all of whom commented on earlier versions of our work.

A number of people outside of RAND also gave freely of their time and talents to review and critique our work. Frank Lacroix, Vice Admiral, U.S. Navy (Retired), now with Science Applications International, provided a thoughtful review of the report. Michael O'Hanlon of the Brookings Institution organized a panel of experts from Brookings to review our briefing and also commented extensively on the draft. E. B. Vandiver, director of the Army's Concepts Analysis Agency (CAA), along with members of his staff, reviewed our work. Price Bingham, formerly of the USAF and now with Northrop-Grumman, offered a number of helpful comments that strengthened the analysis.

Finally, John Godges and Jeanne Heller expertly reviewed and edited the text.

Chapter One

INTRODUCTION: DEFENSE PLANNING
FOR THE 21st CENTURY

It has become commonplace to observe that U.S. military forces are experiencing a period of rapid and profound change. Three important factors that determine the size and characteristics of military forces have changed markedly over the past decade and remain in flux:

- With the collapse of the Soviet Union, the chief threat to U.S. national security no longer stems from a superpower adversary but rather from a handful of hostile or potentially hostile regional powers.

- U.S. forces can expect to face opponents armed with capabilities different from those of our Cold War adversary. Our most likely opponents today field forces with modest numbers of weapons, many of which are a generation or more behind the state of the art; but the prospect is for fairly rapid modernization in selected capabilities.

- Rapid technological advances in such areas as sensors, information processing, and materials are making possible radically new operational concepts that can allow U.S. forces to accomplish their missions in new ways and with far greater levels of efficiency and effectiveness.

Defense planning in the United States has yet to come to grips with the full implications of these far-reaching changes. Within the Department of Defense (DoD), neither resource allocation patterns nor investment priorities have changed much since the 1980s: With some exceptions, the United States is providing somewhat "less of the same" basic forces that it has fielded for the past several decades. And while selected elements of the force, such as battlefield sensors, precision weapons, and stealthy air vehicles, have undergone spectacular improvements in recent years, many think the basic division of labor among joint forces remains essentially the same as it has been for decades.

This is not necessarily wrong: Military missions and the capabilities required to achieve them have a certain enduring quality. For centuries, states have called upon their military forces to defend their borders, to deter adversaries and reassure friends, to impose order on unruly elements, and to act as agents of influence abroad. Yet from time to time, we have seen profound transformations in the tools and, hence, the concepts and strategies with which these missions are accomplished. The most important finding of the research documented in this volume is that U.S. forces are now in the midst of such a historic transformation. The pace of that transformation and, more important, the ability of future U.S. forces to perform their assigned missions will depend critically on the resources that are devoted to the development, testing, and fielding of new systems and concepts.

Just as many observers note the vast change in the defense planning environment, so too do many call for accelerated innovation in U.S. military forces. Calls for a "revolution in military affairs"—within which systems, doctrines, and organizations for warfare would be fundamentally transformed—are legion. The goal of this study is to go beyond advocating change and innovation for their own sake and to base arguments for new capabilities on a set of quantitative and qualitative assessments of future operational needs and opportunities. Without such assessments, arguments for one course of action over another become little more than a competition among judgments or opinions without the possibility of replication or meaningful comparison.

The assessments offered here are of two broad types:

- First, using a novel and fairly transparent quantitative approach we estimate the ability of forces employing advanced firepower to attrit and halt an invading mechanized ground force. This analysis constitutes the centerpiece of the study.

- Second, we incorporate and summarize results from other relevant assessments to evaluate supporting or ancillary aspects of the "halt" campaign. Some of these assessments were made to support this study, others were adapted for this effort.

In both cases, the assessments are presented in the context of future operational needs, as determined from an examination of representative scenarios and alternative strategies for coping with them.

APPROACH AND OVERVIEW

In Chapter Two, we describe a prudent and appropriate generic scenario for assessing the capabilities of U.S. forces in future theater conflicts. In Chapter Three, we digress briefly to describe two alternative, competing concepts for theater military operations that seem to be held currently by U.S. military professionals and defense planners. Chapter Four presents our approach to assessing the capabilities of joint forces to halt armored invasions, as well as the results from applying that approach to a series of different cases within our generic scenario. Chapter Five offers our views on investment priorities as informed by the scenario analysis. Finally, in Chapter Six we suggest the implications for the overall U.S. defense program, including which types of capabilities merit special attention and support and which types might be reduced.

The focus of this analysis is on forces and capabilities needed for large-scale power projection and theater warfare. This focus is appropriate even though U.S. forces are most often engaged in other activities, such as normal training, conducting routine operations abroad to project influence and stability, enforcing international norms on recalcitrant states, combating terrorism, protecting U.S. citizens and others overseas, and providing humanitarian assistance.[1] Nevertheless, the ultimate purpose of U.S. forces—and the

----

[1] For an assessment of the implications of ongoing routine operations for sizing overall U.S. forces, see Paul K. Davis and Richard L. Kugler, "New Principles for Force Sizing," in *Strategic Appraisal 1997: Strategy and Defense Planning for the 21st Century*, RAND, MR-826-AF, 1997, pp. 95–140. For a detailed examination of implications for the United States Air Force, see David E. Thaler and Daniel M. Norton, *Air Force Operations Overseas in Peacetime: OPTEMPO and Force Structure Implications*, RAND, DB-237-AF, 1998.

one for which the bulk of the U.S. force structure is fielded—is to defend the United States and its interests against attack. North Korea, Iraq, Iran, Libya, and other states continue to espouse objectives antithetical to those of the United States and its allies, and these hostile states field military forces that are seen as threatening by neighboring states. In the future other, more powerful states might also adopt objectives and strategies fundamentally at odds with our own. In many cases, only the United States can provide the military power needed to prevent intimidation and deter aggression by adversary states.

The capability for large-scale power projection is what sets the U.S. military establishment apart from every other military in the world today. And it is that ability that allows the United States to credibly underwrite its treaty commitments. Sustaining the capability to defeat major aggression far from our own shores is therefore essential if the United States is to continue to play a leading role in shaping the international security environment. Hence, assessing U.S. forces in terms of their ability to defeat large-scale aggression is properly the main (albeit not the sole) focus of defense planning.

Chapter Two

SCENARIOS FOR EVALUATING FUTURE NEEDS AND CAPABILITIES

The beginning of wisdom in defense planning is an appreciation of the great degree to which the scenarios employed in the planning process can shape the outcome. Since the development of the Base Force in the early 1990s, two scenarios depicting major theater wars (MTWs)—a North Korean attack on the Republic of Korea, and an Iraqi attack on Kuwait and Saudi Arabia—have been virtually the sole focus of force planning in the Department of Defense.[1] To an extent that was probably neither anticipated nor intended by the DoD leadership at the time, these two scenarios (and, more precisely, certain carefully defined cases within them) have constricted the focus of force planning efforts to a fairly narrow portion of the spectrum of plausible challenges U.S. forces might face. Thus, U.S. defense planning may be giving short shrift to some important factors that should be considered in evaluating future needs.

The problem is not that these two canonical scenarios are not useful. On the contrary, their primary features (but not their details) represent the most plausible near-term threats of large-scale attack that

---

[1]DoD did employ a range of other scenarios during its 1997 Quadrennial Defense Review. Other scenarios included situations in which an adversary with larger and more capable forces than those portrayed in the MTWs attacked U.S. and allied forces. DoD also used a series of smaller-scale operations as well as MTWs to assess overall force needs in its "Dynamic Commitment" series of exercises. However, the "near peer" assessments were fairly limited in scope and seemed to have little influence in the resource allocation process. The Dynamic Commitment effort did not attempt to go beyond informed judgment with regard to the types and number of forces needed in each of its scenarios. See William S. Cohen, *Report of the Quadrennial Defense Review,* U.S. Department of Defense, May 1997, p. 24. See also Les Aspin, *Report of the Bottom-Up Review,* U.S. Department of Defense, October 1993, pp. 13–15.

U.S. forces face. The Persian Gulf scenario—in which a regional adversary with a mix of 1970s, 1980s, and 1990s weaponry attacks its badly outnumbered neighbors—is representative of a range of challenges that could confront U.S. forces in the future. And both scenarios are credible: There is little room for doubt that these are wars that the United States would fight if they broke out. Nevertheless, in and of themselves, these two scenarios, as used by DoD, are not adequate yardsticks against which to measure current and future U.S. military capabilities. The reasons are manifold.

First, the military challenges posed in each of the two scenarios, as officially described, are too easily dealt with to serve as a basis for prudent planning (see Figure 2.1). As was revealed in a study of the heavy bomber force in 1995, the canonical scenario for the Persian Gulf region assumes that U.S. forces will have nearly two weeks' re-

RAND*MR958-2.1*

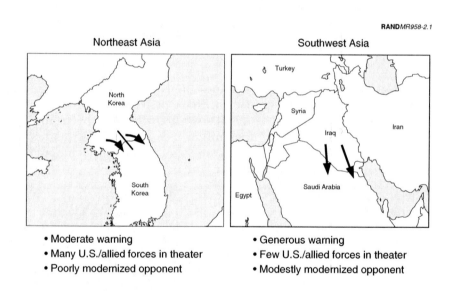

Northeast Asia

Southwest Asia

• Moderate warning
• Many U.S./allied forces in theater
• Poorly modernized opponent

• Generous warning
• Few U.S./allied forces in theater
• Modestly modernized opponent

Figure 2.1—Canonical Scenarios Do Not Pose a Stressing Challenge

inforcement time prior to the commencement of hostilities.[2] During this period, the United States would be able to send more than a dozen fighter squadrons, two to three brigades of Army and Marine forces, and two to three carrier battle groups to the theater. Other U.S. forces would continue to arrive during the course of the campaign. Not surprisingly, assessments of the outcome of such a conflict show U.S. and allied forces winning handily. But what rational adversary would wait to attack under such unfavorable circumstances? If potential adversaries learned anything from the Gulf War, it was that they must strike before the United States deploys large-scale forces to their region and that they must do all they can to impede the progress of that deployment once it begins.

Moreover, history shows that the wars that U.S. forces fight are not the ones for which they prepare and deploy promptly. Several wars did not happen—the Taiwan Strait, Korea (post-1953), and, perhaps, Central Europe throughout the Cold War—at least in part because of prompt or sustained U.S. deployments. Korea (1950) and Iraq's attack on Kuwait, on the other hand, suggest that a failure to anticipate or to react promptly to threats of aggression may invite attack. Prudence therefore dictates that the scenarios used to test U.S. defense preparedness include the possibility of surprise. Improved monitoring capabilities and a vigilant attitude can reduce the probability of U.S. forces having to defend from an unreinforced posture, but they cannot ensure that warning indicators will always be acted upon. Prompt action often depends not only on the speed of decisionmaking in Washington but also on the cooperation of U.S. allies and friends. Building a consensus for action can take time. In short, a defense posture that relies for its viability on a lengthy period of reinforcement would be a poor deterrent and would subject U.S. forces and interests to substantial and unnecessary risks.

A second way in which the canonical cases are insufficiently challenging is in their assumptions regarding the enemy's use of existing or emerging attack capabilities. The scenarios appear to be fairly sanguine about the possibility that U.S. forces might come under at-

---

[2]See Paul G. Kaminski, *Heavy Bomber Force Study* (Briefing Charts), U.S. Department of Defense, 1995.

tack by large numbers of ballistic and cruise missiles, some of which could deliver chemical, biological, or nuclear weapons.

It is widely recognized that our most plausible adversaries today—including North Korea, Iran, and Iraq—have stocks of lethal chemical agents. It should also be assumed that despite our best efforts to the contrary, over the next ten years or so, fission weapons will be in the hands of a larger number of countries than today.[3] In its Quadrennial Defense Review of 1996–1997, DoD recognized the need to enhance U.S. forces' ability to withstand chemical and biological attacks. And while spending on protective gear is increasing, force structure and operational concepts seem not to have been affected. Similarly, in most DoD analyses, naval forces appear to have had unimpeded access to favorable operating areas inside the Gulf, despite the likelihood that future adversaries will invest in more-advanced anti-ship cruise missiles, mines, and, in Iran's case, submarines.

The combination of these rather optimistic assumptions—generous warning time for reinforcement and low risk of attack by long-range missiles or other capable weapons—sets the stage for official assessments that understate the importance of reposturing U.S. forces or providing them with new capabilities to offset growth in the future attack capabilities of adversaries. As we shall see, a shorter-warning scenario in the Gulf would show the benefits from strengthening U.S. prepositioned forces and assets there and procuring larger numbers of advanced munitions and other enhancements. Likewise, any assessment that credits adversaries with plausible capabilities to attack U.S. forces with ballistic or antiship missiles would highlight the need for theater missile defenses and longer-range attack assets. By contrast, the use of "watered-down" scenarios tends to emphasize force size over innovation.[4]

---

[3]For an overview of the current and projected status of chemical, biological, and nuclear threats to U.S. interests, see *Strategic Assessment 1995*, National Defense University Institute for International Strategic Studies, U.S. Government Printing Office, Washington, D.C., 1995.

[4]Prior RAND work has demonstrated the importance of "capabilities analysis" across a wide range of scenarios and cases within scenarios. For a summary of recent RAND work, see Paul Davis, Richard Hillestad, and Natalie Crawford, "Capabilities for Major Regional Conflicts," in Zalmay Khalilzad and David Ochmanek (eds.), *Strategic Appraisal '97*, RAND, 1997, pp. 141–178. An important conclusion of this work is that

A GENERIC SCENARIO FOR FORCE PLANNING

Prudence demands that we measure U.S. forces against the challenges that could be posed by representative adversaries that are reasonably competent and fairly well equipped. Accordingly, the analysis that follows is based largely on the challenges, objectives, and constraints that arise in the scenario outlined in Figure 2.2.

In positing this generic scenario, we recognize that regional adversaries generally do not need to defeat the United States and its armed forces in order to achieve their objectives. In the main, our adversaries in the post–Cold War environment seek to undermine U.S. influence in their regions so that they may have a greater say in that region's affairs. This means that limited objectives—coercing neighboring states or seizing key territory or assets—might well serve to

RAND*MR958*-2.2

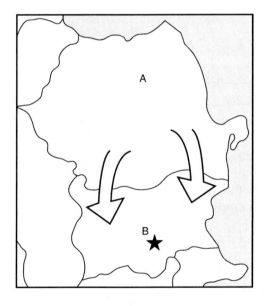

- Enemy objectives
  - Seize vital assets
  - Undermine U.S. influence
  - Dominate the region
- Enemy approach
  - Attack with little warning
  - Move with maximum speed
  - Deter/impede U.S. access
    - Air and missile attacks
    - Weapons of mass destruction
    - Countermaritime access

Figure 2.2—Adversaries Will Seek to Achieve and Exploit Surprise

---

U.S. forces may suffer from growing shortfalls, the most important of which are associated with mounting effective operations early in short-warning conflicts.

meet the adversary's objectives. And it means these adversaries will avoid a major engagement with U.S. forces, if they can.

The above, coupled with the realities that our adversaries will fight close to home and can generally be confident of having the initiative in the opening phase of a future war, suggests an enemy approach that relies on surprise, speed of maneuver, and efforts to impede U.S. access to the region and to suppress the U.S. tempo of operations. As noted above, a range of military capabilities well suited to this approach is available to potential enemies.

While all of this might seem obvious, it is worth noting again that much of the work supporting DoD's program reviews downplays these very factors. Moreover, an approach that recognizes the inherent asymmetries in the strategic and operational situations of the United States and its potential enemies renders moot many of the arguments opposing certain new systems currently under DoD development. Some critics of ongoing modernization efforts seem to believe that if they can establish that a particular U.S. system under development is substantially more capable than those that will be possessed by our adversaries, they will have made the case that the system is "not needed." Such judgments are too often based on simple system-versus-system comparisons that neglect the taxing circumstances under which U.S. forces frequently must operate.

An approach to force planning that encompasses strategic and operational asymmetries reveals that, in selected areas, U.S. forces may need capabilities far superior to those fielded by their opponents in order to prevail in future conflicts as quickly and as effectively as is called for by U.S. strategy. Projecting military power on short notice into the "back yard" of a major regional power is an inherently demanding enterprise, particularly when that enemy is willing to accept vastly more casualties than the intervening outside power. This situation places a high premium on forces that can deploy rapidly, seize the initiative, and achieve their objectives with minimal risk of heavy casualties. Only by using plausibly stressing scenarios as the yardstick against which to measure the capabilities of future U.S. military forces can the importance of innovation and modernization be given fair weight.

Figure 2.3 fleshes out our generic scenario; it depicts the forces that a typical regional adversary (e.g., Iran or Iraq) might bring to bear in the middle or later years of the next decade.[5] These forces include several army corps (including 12 heavy armor or mechanized divisions), upwards of 500 combat aircraft (a portion of which would be of recent manufacture), chemical and biological weapons, and tactical and theater-range ballistic and cruise missiles. A more sizable nation, such as China, could certainly commit a larger force against its neighbors, though qualitatively the threat would look much the same. We judge this time frame—roughly ten years in the future—to be best suited as a basis for informing choices about today's defense program, because it is set far enough in the future to account for lead times in fielding systems currently under development yet is near enough to the present to permit us to

RAND*MR958-2.3*

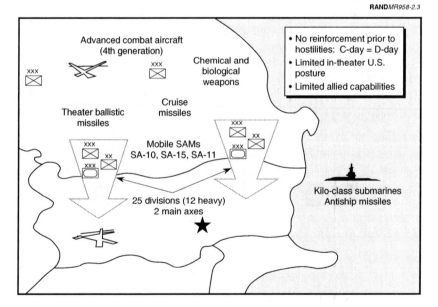

Figure 2.3—A Representative Scenario for Force Planning

---

[5]Aspin, 1993, pp. 13–15.

forecast with some confidence such factors as the U.S. regional posture and adversary objectives and capabilities.

In broad terms, we assume that the enemy's chief objective is to seize critical assets some distance from the prewar border. Hence, mechanized ground forces spearheading the enemy advance are instructed to move as rapidly as possible. We also assume that the enemy is capable of a combined air and land operation, with reasonably modern surface-to-air defenses, interceptors, and attack aircraft. Most important, we assume that, for one reason or another, U.S. forces have not substantially reinforced the theater prior to the attack. In the vernacular, C-day (the day that large-scale U.S. reinforcement begins) equals D-day (the day that the enemy commences his attack). This could happen if U.S. indications and warning assets fail to detect or correctly assess enemy preparations for an attack, if U.S. decisionmakers delay reacting to warning, or if the leaders of countries threatened by the attack temporize in allowing U.S. forces access to their territory in the face of ambiguous indications of hostile intent. Assumptions about the employment of specific forces and systems are discussed in detail in Chapter Four, which presents our assessment of potential U.S. halt capabilities.

This case represents a stressing challenge for the defenders, even if weapons of mass destruction (WMD) are not used in support of the attack. Nevertheless, this case does not represent a "worst case." In August 1990, the order to deploy U.S. combat forces to the Gulf came four days *after* Iraqi forces marched into Kuwait.[6] If Saddam had chosen a more aggressive strategy, the first U.S. forces to arrive in theater could have found themselves fighting an enemy already well into Saudi Arabia. If one accepts the possibility of such an eventuality, the issue becomes whether and how such an attack might be defeated. The next chapter describes two contrasting approaches to defeating a heavily armored offensive.

----

[6]*Conduct of the Persian Gulf War*, U.S. Department of Defense, Washington, D.C., April 1992, p. 35.

Chapter Three

COMPETING APPROACHES TO THEATER WARFARE

Increasingly, it is possible to divide U.S. military professionals and defense planners into two schools of thought regarding future theater warfare. In fact, many of the issues debated within DoD over the past few years—such as the calibration of combat simulation models, the proper allocation of airlift assets among different force elements, appropriate future force size and mix, and weapons investment priorities—are, to a large degree, manifestations of underlying differences between these two schools of thought. This chapter reviews this emerging debate to set the context for the analysis that follows.

Figure 3.1 illustrates, in simplified fashion, a traditional approach to theater warfare. Forces are arrayed opposite one another on the battlefield prior to the initiation of conflict. The attacker chooses the time and place of attack.

The defender, unsure of his ability to anticipate where the main blow will come and unwilling or unable to give up ground while he sizes up the situation, is compelled to distribute his forces forward in a linear fashion. The mission of the forward defending units is to slow and attrit the attacking forces, to direct longer-range fires in support of the defense, and to confirm the location of main thrusts and potential enemy breakthroughs. Operational reserves in the defender's rear area plug gaps where breakthroughs have occurred and threaten "counterstroke" attacks.

This operational concept, which is reminiscent of Europe's Central Front during much of the Cold War but broadly representative of land combat for centuries, is imposed upon the defender by two main factors:

RAND*MR958-3.1*

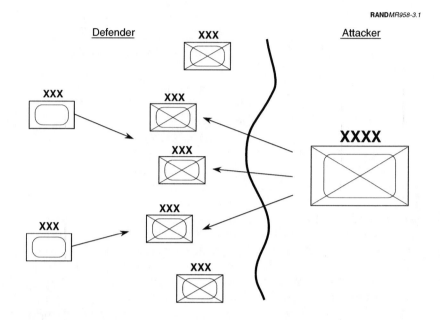

Figure 3.1—Past Warfighting Concepts Focused on the Close Battle

- The first (which has already been mentioned) is the defender's inability to know with confidence where and when the enemy might strike with his main thrust(s), thus compelling the defender to be prepared to fight along a broad front.

- Second, the bulk of the firepower used to destroy enemy formations is fielded in short-range, direct-fire weapons, such as tank guns and antitank guided missiles, which are effective only at line-of-sight ranges. Longer-range fires, such as those provided by artillery and aircraft, are seen as useful in suppressing enemy activities, delaying movement, and so forth, but not in attriting enemy armor. For this reason, the close battle is necessarily seen as the decisive point in conflicts. Longer-range fires have been confined to a supporting role.

When applied to the United States' strategic situation, such an approach to warfare demands that large numbers of U.S. heavy ground forces (or capable allied ground forces) be deployed abroad in areas threatened by short-notice attack. This approach also demands that the population and leadership of the United States be prepared to accept fairly heavy casualties in the event of war. As countless battles between armored opponents have shown, close battles are inherently dangerous for participants on both sides when undertaken by forces of roughly equal capability.

This approach to theater warfare was appropriate for the United States during the Cold War. Interests of sufficient gravity were at stake to merit the stationing of more than six U.S. heavy divisions in Central Europe. Likewise, all sides recognized that war in Europe, if it came, would entail heavy casualties and incalculable risks. NATO was never able to approach the Warsaw Pact in terms of numbers of troops and weapons deployed, and so relied on the advantages of the defender and the possibility of escalation to nuclear use to deter serious attempts at aggression or coercion by Moscow. In any case, there was no realistic alternative: NATO could not afford to trade much space for time. As long as friendly forces were not able both to conduct effective reconnaissance deep behind enemy lines and to rapidly apply effective firepower against enemy armored forces at extended ranges, a credible defense posture depended upon having heavy forces based forward.

Today, however, almost everything has changed. The United States no longer routinely stations massive forces abroad in the regions where its interests are most exposed to threats of aggression—the Persian Gulf and Korea. In the Gulf, this results in part from the need to respect the views of host country governments that wish to minimize the impact of the U.S. military presence on their cultural and political institutions. In Korea, it results in part from the impressive and growing defensive capabilities of our ally, the Republic of Korea. In both cases, it results also from economic considerations: Stationing large numbers of forces abroad, especially ground forces, is manpower intensive, and manpower is expensive. Equally important, neither U.S. leaders nor the electorate seem prepared to accept the necessity of taking heavy casualties in order to defeat aggression in these or other theaters.

The problem is that readily available U.S. forces may not be capable of defeating a large-scale, combined-arms offensive under some conditions. With current operational strategy and investment priorities, DoD is, in effect, applying a traditional approach to defeating armored attacks when fundamental elements of that approach—heavy forward stationing and casualty tolerance—are missing. The disjuncture between U.S. means and ends is especially pronounced in the Gulf, where indigenous friendly forces are badly outnumbered and, hence, may not be sufficient to mount a large-scale defensive effort of their own.

Figure 3.2 shows what happens when a traditional approach to warfare and a traditional means of assessing combat outcomes are applied to a fundamentally new situation. The line marked "Enemy advance" shows the rate at which enemy ground forces could advance under our scenario assumptions when moving over fairly open terrain and against forces that might be encountered in the Persian Gulf region. Their progress, as marked on the left vertical

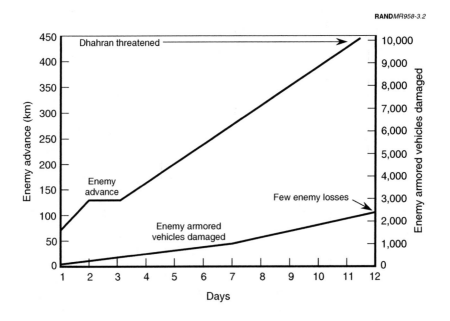

Figure 3.2—Traditional Concepts Fail in Stressing Cases: Persian Gulf Scenario, C-day = D-day

axis, shows they might be capable of overrunning Ras Tenura, Dhahran, and other critical economic objectives in less than two weeks.

One reason for this outcome is that U.S. forces are judged unable to attrit leading elements of the attacking force rapidly enough to allow the sparse U.S. and allied ground forces to compel them to halt in a close battle.[1]

Fortunately, key factors bearing on the outcome of this hypothetical battle are changing in favor of the United States. Emerging technologies are supporting new systems and concepts that can allow U.S. forces both to "see deep" (that is, into the opponent's operational second echelon) and to "kill deep." Future U.S. and allied commanders should be able to know with a high degree of confidence when and where large-scale enemy armored forces are moving. Armed with that knowledge, commanders should be able to direct highly effective firepower assets not only to slow and disrupt enemy columns but also to rapidly impose high levels of attrition.

This emerging concept of operations is sketched in Figure 3.3. Here, information and firepower perform many aspects of the roles formerly played by mechanized defensive ground forces in the defense. Most significantly, the lion's share of the enemy's maneuver forces is engaged and destroyed not in the close battle but by longer-range fires. Rather than acting as the primary means of reconnaissance and attrition, defending armored formations in the opening "halt" phase of a theater campaign now perform three main tasks:

- By their very presence in the theater in peacetime (through prepositioning or, preferably, forward stationing), the formations ensure that the enemy cannot seize critical objectives without committing sizable mechanized forces to the offensive. Heavily armored forces, along with their accompanying logistics train, move more slowly than lighter forces can.

---

[1]Note that the allied forces are assessed as being able to destroy or damage some 2400 of the enemy's nearly 10,000 attacking armored vehicles in 12 days. This is not a bad result by historical standards, but it would clearly be insufficient in this scenario if the enemy were determined to press the attack.

RAND*MR958-3.3*

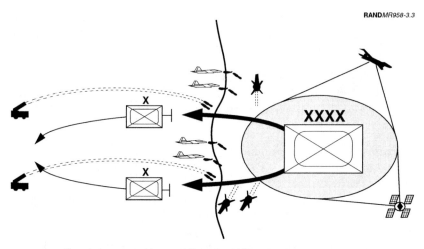

• Terrain is covered by surveillance and firepower
• Longer-range fires do not just disrupt, they attrit
• Ground forces compel the enemy to commit large mechanized
  forces and provide blocking when force ratios are favorable

Figure 3.3—Emerging Concept for Halting Invasions

•   The formations provide a "backstop" function, preparing to en-
    gage enemy units that might be reconstituted or slip through al-
    lied fires intact.

•   And, if necessary, friendly ground forces can employ delay and
    retrograde tactics, exploiting superior battlefield information and
    mobility to block temporarily the advance elements of the
    attacking force. Such operations can be risky, but they can
    compel the attackers to slow down at points well short of their
    objectives and may create more lucrative targets for allied fires.

Before we examine this emerging approach as it applies to theater
warfare, Figure 3.4 provides a glimpse at some key capabilities that
have been fielded to make this concept a reality. The lowest line on
the figure shows our assessment of the effectiveness of 1970s-era
fixed wing aircraft and weapons in locating and destroying enemy
maneuver forces. Using route reconnaissance tactics and cued by
reports from friendly ground forces, aircraft such as the F-4E would
rely chiefly on the human eye to locate and engage moving armor,

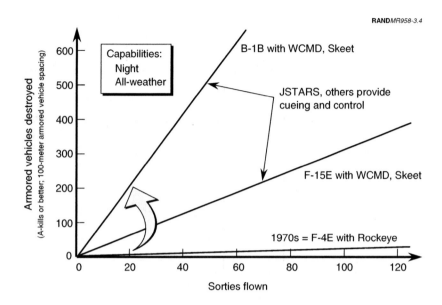

Figure 3.4—Emerging Firepower and Information Capabilities Enable a
New Approach to Theater Warfare

resulting in many sorties that failed to locate and engage enemy ground forces. Those sorties that did engage valid armored targets would, in a high-threat environment, deliver an unguided antiarmor cluster weapon, such as the Mk-20 Rockeye. Under these conditions and given the limitations of those weapons, several sorties would be required, on average, to achieve a high degree of confidence of killing a single armored vehicle. At night or in poor weather, sortie effectiveness—already quite low—declined markedly.

Contrast that operational concept with the capabilities of forces and assets being fielded today: Airborne surveillance platforms—such as the E-8 Joint Surveillance and Target Attack Radar System (JSTARS) carrying moving target indication (MTI) and other radar sensors— can detect moving vehicles at ranges of one hundred miles or more. Soon these assets will be supplemented by other platforms, such as unmanned aerial vehicles (UAVs) carrying multispectral imaging sensors. Together, such sensors will give commanders and control centers an accurate picture of the movements of large-scale mechanized formations in near-real time. Controllers can use this information to direct attack assets rapidly to the most important and lucrative targets. Weapons such as the wind-corrected munitions dispenser (WCMD) and the Army Tactical Missile System (ATACMS) can accurately deliver large numbers of smart, antiarmor submunitions, such as the BLU-108 sensor fuzed weapon (also called SFW or "Skeet") and the Brilliant Anti-Tank (BAT) weapon. Such weapons have demonstrated a level of lethality against moving armor that is an order of magnitude or more greater than earlier-generation area munitions, such as Rockeye.

Thus, compared with our capabilities of a decade or more ago, many more of our long-range attack assets will find their targets, and those attacks will be vastly more effective. Moreover, because the new long-range sensors and specialized munitions are not degraded in conditions of poor visibility, enemy maneuver forces will have no sanctuary at night or in bad weather.

These emerging capabilities could fundamentally transform the way that U.S. forces fight wars against mechanized opponents. Under many conditions, enemy maneuver forces now can be engaged and neutralized before those forces have the chance to close with friendly ground forces. And with rapidly deployable firepower assets, such as fighter and bomber aircraft, playing a major role in destroying enemy armored forces, the United States should be able to protect its interests and its allies with relatively modest forces stationed and deployed abroad in peacetime.

Naturally, concepts relying upon standoff surveillance and advanced firepower are best suited to situations in which enemy forces must move across fairly open or channelized terrain in large numbers to achieve their objectives. Other situations will arise, particularly in smaller-scale conflicts, where enemy forces—perhaps infantry or irregular troops on foot and in urban or heavily forested terrain—would be far less vulnerable to this sort of approach.[2] Nevertheless, deterring and defeating attacks by large-scale armored forma-

---

[2]For an in-depth assessment of the roles that modern air forces can play in defeating smaller-scale aggression, see Alan Vick, David Orletsky, Abram Shulsky, and John Stillion, *Preparing the U.S. Air Force for Military Operations Other Than War*, RAND, MR-842-AF, 1997.

tions remain important objectives—perhaps the most important objectives—assigned to U.S. military forces. With the proper levels of attention and investment, U.S. forces have the potential to render this form of warfare virtually obsolete for our opponents.

Writing more than a decade ago, the British armor officer and military theorist Richard Simpkin concluded that "the dominance of indirect fire achieved by surveillance and fire control on the one hand, and by terminal guidance on the other [means that] whether they are in armored vehicles, on their feet, or dug in, troops deployed at high density will certainly be pulverized into incapacity and . . . destroyed."[3] Simpkin recognized that changes in capabilities of this magnitude imply the need for an equally fundamental revision of operational concepts, force mix, and investment strategy. This study seeks to inform those revisions.

---

[3]Richard E. Simpkin, *Race to the Swift*, Brassey's Defence Publishers, London, 1985, p. 50.

Chapter Four

ASSESSING FUTURE U.S. CAPABILITIES FOR THE HALT PHASE

Current U.S. defense strategy recognizes that success or failure in future theater conflicts will hinge largely on the outcome of the opening phase of the campaign—what has come to be called the "halt" phase. The *Report of the Quadrennial Defense Review* notes that maintaining the capability "to rapidly defeat enemy advances short of their objectives . . . is absolutely critical to the United States' ability to seize the initiative . . . and to minimize the amount of territory we and our allies must regain."[1]

This emphasis on success in the opening phase is appropriate: If U.S. and allied forces are able to halt the attacking force short of its primary objectives, the remainder of the conflict is likely to unfold along favorable lines. Having halted the attack, the allied coalition will have gone far toward seizing the initiative from the enemy. Coalition forces should also find it easier to secure important rear-area assets, such as airfields and ports, needed to facilitate the arrival of follow-on reinforcements and supplies. By halting the attack short of its primary objectives, the United States and its allies will have denied the enemy its most important potential bargaining asset. Failure to halt the attack, by contrast, would mean a war of incalculably greater cost, risk, and duration. Finally, an allied force that is postured to effect a halt quickly is likely to serve as a robust deterrent to a potentially aggressive state.

---

[1]William S. Cohen, Secretary of Defense, *Report of the Quadrennial Defense Review,* U.S. Department of Defense, Washington, D.C., May 1997, p. 13.

The basic elements of the scenario used in this analysis are outlined
in Chapter Two. Figure 4.1 shows key assumptions of our base case.
We assume a U.S. posture that could be characterized as "Southern
Watch plus."[2] That is, U.S. forces in the region at the commencement of combat are somewhat more robust than those deployed today in the Gulf Region. They consist of five squadrons of land-based
aircraft, prepositioned equipment for two heavy Army brigades, a
battalion of 24 AH-64 Apache helicopters, a carrier battle group, and
250 ATACMS missiles, mounted either on Multiple Launch Rocket
System (MLRS) launchers or, as has been proposed, Navy surface

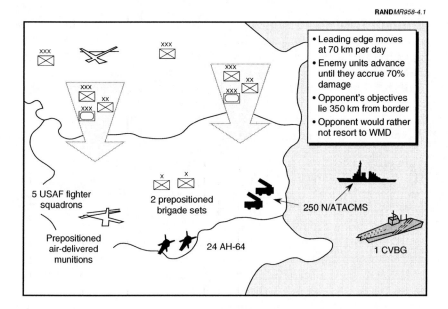

RANDMR958-4.1

Figure 4.1—Base Case Assumptions

---

[2]Southern Watch is the name given to allied operations in the Persian Gulf region
aimed at monitoring Iraqi military activities and deterring potential aggression against
the states of the Gulf Cooperation Council.

combatants afloat in the region. We also assume in this base case that all air-to-ground munitions are prepositioned at multiple locations and can be distributed to main operating bases by intratheater airlift and surface transportation.

Assumptions about the employment of available forces are as important as the number and capabilities of those forces. We assume that the enemy's chief objective is to seize critical assets some distance from the prewar border. Hence, mechanized ground forces spearheading the enemy advance are instructed to move as rapidly as possible. We assume that the leading edge of those forces moves at an average rate of approximately 70 kilometers per day.[3] We assume as well that each unit moving forward will sustain this average velocity until that unit—be it a platoon, a company, or a battalion—suffers the loss of some 70 percent of its armored vehicles. This assumption is based on a deliberately conservative judgment of the level of attrition required to render an attacking force incapable of coherent offensive operation. We also assume that the enemy uses its air defenses to try to protect this advancing force. That is, mobile surface-to-air missiles (SAMs) advance along with the leading edge of the attacking ground force, and interceptors operate from time to time within this same airspace.[4]

Our base case assumes that the enemy possesses but does not use lethal chemical, biological, or nuclear weapons in the halt phase—not because such use can be ruled out but rather because most ad-

---

[3]In actuality, a large enemy force will move at an uneven rate—faster at the outset of an operation and slower after a few days, when its fuel and other consumables are depleted and supply lines lengthen. In any case, 70 km per day is a rate of advance far greater than that achieved by most modern armies in actual combat. However, we are interested in estimating the progress of the leading edge of the enemy ground force in the face of modest opposing ground forces. Given major lines of communication of limited capacity, a rate of some 70 kilometers per day is required in order to move the overall force—its centroid—at a slower rate of around 30 kilometers per day. Thirty kilometers per day is, in fact, on the high side of historical examples for the movement of the forward edge of the battle area (FEBA) when large-scale mechanized forces are attacking against some resistance. The Germans' mechanized forces moving through France in 1940, for example, covered 220 miles (350 kilometers) in 20 days, or 18 kilometers per day on average. J.F.C. Fuller, *A Military History of the Western World*, Vol. 3, Funk and Wagnalls, New York, 1956, p. 396.

[4]Such a doctrine risks some fratricide, but it provides the enemy with the best prospect of limiting damage to its ground forces from U.S. and allied air forces.

versaries would prefer to achieve their objectives without running the risks associated with first use of such weapons. In this case, the enemy reserves weapons of mass destruction as a means for helping to ensure the survival of his regime should the war turn bad. Later in this chapter we offer an assessment of the effects of early and large-scale use of such weapons by the enemy, as well as evaluations of cases in which other parameters assumed above are changed.

EMPLOYING THE FORCE: FIRST ENABLE, THEN DESTROY

There is more to halting an armored invasion than simply killing tanks. In order to deploy forces of sufficient size into the theater with acceptable risk and to employ that force effectively, U.S. and allied forces must gain a measure of control over other enemy military capabilities. Therefore to defeat an enemy attack, we first focus on gaining a foothold in the theater and creating favorable conditions under which U.S. and allied forces can operate. This is the "enabling" portion of the halt phase. We then focus on destroying enemy armored columns as rapidly as possible.

Key objectives in the enabling portion of the halt phase are to

- protect rear-area assets (airfields, logistics centers, ports, allied population and industrial centers) from attacks by aircraft, missiles, and special operations forces,

- suppress and destroy enemy air defenses, including the most-capable interceptors and surface-to-air missile systems,

- disrupt enemy command, control, and communications as well as transportation networks through precision attacks on fixed targets, such as command posts, communication nodes, key bridges, and choke points, and

- destroy weapons of mass destruction whenever they can be located.

Assets to accomplish these objectives would be those in-theater prior to the outbreak of hostilities, as well as those that could arrive within the first few days after C-day. Notable among these are F-15Cs, F-22s, and multirole aircraft for air defense and sweeps against enemy aircraft; the airborne laser system, Aegis upper tier, and

Patriot or other land-based ballistic missile defense systems; B-2s, to destroy the most capable of the enemy's SAM systems with attacks by medium-range standoff weapons; F-18s and F-16s carrying high-speed antiradiation (HARM) missiles to suppress other SAM radars; and systems—notably the stealthy F-117 attack aircraft, and the Tomahawk land attack missile (TLAM), joint air-to-surface standoff missile (JASSM), and conventional air-launched cruise missile (CALCM) cruise missiles—for precision attacks on fixed, often hardened targets.

During these first few days of the defensive operation, modest numbers of assets could be assigned to attack the leading edges of armored columns. ATACMS missiles delivering BAT submunitions would be especially useful if they were within range, because they can be employed effectively before many of the enemy's mobile air defenses have been neutralized. Attack helicopters and fixed-wing aircraft such as the A-10 would also be pressed into service to attack formations in areas where air defenses had been partially suppressed.

Not until the enabling phase has been under way for some time—in our assessment of this scenario, four to five days—would the bulk of the assets be turned toward attacks on the enemy's armored columns. Given a relatively modern and reasonably well-employed enemy air defense system, it would take about this long before non-stealthy aircraft, such as the B-1B and the F-15E, could operate at medium altitudes with relative safety. Once the enemy's interceptor and SAM forces had been effectively suppressed, however, these and other platforms can bring massive amounts of firepower to bear.

Table 4.1 shows the flow of U.S. firepower assets to the theater over the first 12 days of the war. This arrival rate assumes that the Civil Reserve Air Fleet (CRAF) Stage II has been activated and that, by Day 4, approximately 900 tons of intertheater airlift capacity are available to support USAF deployments each day.[5] The table shows that the Air Force could expect to deploy about one and a half squadrons

---

[5]This is equivalent to around 40 percent or less of the total airlift capacity available, depending on the distance to deploy, the availability of en-route and in-theater staging bases, crew ratio, tanker availability, and other variables. Were more than 40 percent of the total airlift capacity available, these units could deploy more quickly.

Table 4.1

Assumed Deployment: Base Case, Halt Phase

Day	Forces (fighter aircraft in squadrons) [a]
0 (in-place)	2 ×[b] F-15C, F-16(L), A-10, F-16HTS, 3 × FA-18, 1xBn AH-64, 250 ATACMS
1	F-22, F-117, 8 B-2
2	F-22, 3 × airborne laser
3	F-16HTS, F-15C
4	F-15E
5	F-15E, 50 B-1B aircraft
6	F-16(L)
7	F-16(L), F-15C, 3 × F/A-18 (USN), 2 × F/A-18 (USMC)
8	F-15E
9	F-16(L)
10	2 × F-16
11	O/A-10
12	O/A-10

[a]F-16 (L) refers to F-16 systems equipped with a LANTIRN targeting and navigation pod, and F-16HTS refers to F-16 systems equipped with the HARM targeting system, used for SEAD.
[b]× = units.

of combat aircraft per day to a distant theater under these conditions, assuming the availability of suitable airfields. We also show 50 B-1Bs arriving in the region on Day 5, and a second carrier battle group, along with two squadrons of Marine Corps F-18s, arriving on Day 7. Numerous support aircraft also deploy in this period, including aircraft for reconnaissance (U-2 and RC-135), surveillance and control (AWACS and JSTARS), aerial refueling (KC-135 and KC-10), search and rescue, and intratheater airlift.

Figure 4.2 provides two snapshots that characterize the allocation of available firepower assets on Day 4 and Day 8 of the halt phase. On Day 4, the bulk of the effort is devoted to such enabling tasks as suppression of enemy air defenses (SEAD), air defense and sweep missions (air-to-air), and attacks on high-value and time-sensitive fixed

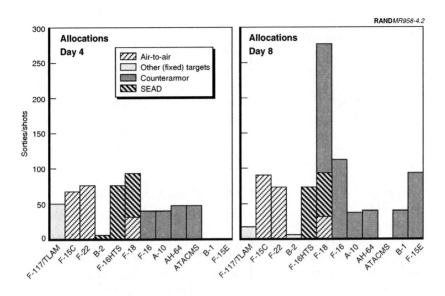

Figure 4.2—Sortie/Missile Apportionments Vary Between Early and Late Halt Phase

targets.[6] By Day 8, more assets are available to the commander, and most of them are devoted to attacking the enemy's advancing armored columns.

ASSESSING A SINGLE OPERATIONAL OBJECTIVE RATHER THAN A THEATER CAMPAIGN

We have specified the initiating conditions and basic forces in the opening phase of a future conflict. Before offering our assessment— that is, before turning these inputs into outputs—some words about methodology are called for. The approach used in this analysis is cast at the operational level, and it focuses on a single operational

---

[6]We assumed that the 250 available N/ATACMS were expended evenly over the first five days of the campaign. Attacks by assets from outside the theater, e.g., B-52s operating from bases in the United States, are not shown.

objective—halting an enemy invasion through direct attacks on armored columns. The great advantage of choosing this fairly narrow focus is that it allows the analyst to employ a fairly simple and straightforward approach (or "model") in assessing the effectiveness of a particular set of forces. Other objectives that bear on this central one—such as deploying forces to the theater, defending rear-area assets, and gaining air superiority—are assessed separately, and the results of those assessments are applied as appropriate.

A more common approach to assessing the capabilities of alternative forces is to use a theater-level simulation model—a large and rather complex computer model of a theater war that encompasses within it many operational objectives. The advantage of this approach is that it can capture quantitatively (albeit at varying levels of fidelity) the interactions among all of the significant facets of the joint campaign. Such a model can be indispensable if one is trying to assess trade-offs among systems and force elements that contribute to dissimilar objectives, such as the value of air defense assets versus airlift versus the protection of sea lines of communication. The drawbacks of such models, however, are considerable: They often combine the worst features of complexity and simplification. Because of their sheer size, theater-level simulation models can be sufficiently complex that the consumer of the analysis (and frequently the analysts themselves) may find it difficult to audit and track the myriad assumptions built into the model. This makes it hard to identify and understand the interactions that are most salient in determining the results. The complexity and configuration of some of the models might require weeks of setup time, even by a well-staffed study team, to configure input data for the model. As a result, the analyst often can run only a small number of excursions around a limited number of scenarios.[7]

For all of this complexity, however, when one looks closely at the individual components of many large models—the air defense and air

---

[7]RAND has developed a theater model called the Joint Integrated Contingency Model (JICM). Its design and relative modernity make it fairly easy to modify and a good candidate for exploratory analysis—where large numbers of cases are considered with variations of force levels, force effectiveness parameters, and so forth. However, even JICM is larger and more complex than what is needed for the problems examined here. Further, JICM currently employs a rather aggregated approach to some of the key phenomena that we are interested examining in detail.

defense suppression portions, for example, or the close air support (CAS) module—one finds that gross simplifications often have been made, both to fill gaps in knowledge about elements of the operation and so that the model will run with a reasonable amount of input data and within a reasonable amount of time. For example, in the version of the TACWAR model used by DoD, the user is not able to focus the most effective SAM suppression assets against the most capable SAM systems or on the most important parts of the battlefield. Many sorties allocated to attacks on enemy ground forces are wasted, because the model allows them to be allocated to sectors of the battlefield that lack suitable targets. Too often these shortcomings are glossed over, both in the assessment of combat and in the presentation of those assessments. The result can be a badly distorted picture of the capabilities and limitations of certain types of forces.

In particular, it is common for today's theater-level models to systematically downplay the contributions of advanced information and firepower systems to the joint battle. That is in part because the theater models most widely used today were developed over the previous 20 years or so. When these models were first conceived, the capabilities of long-range reconnaissance and fire systems were quite limited. Parameters reflecting the effectiveness of these systems were calibrated accordingly and, in many instances, have not been changed to reflect the capabilities of more-modern systems.

Most important, the heart of the TACWAR model is the close battle—tank versus tank—because that was the expected locus of the decisive battle in the major theater wars of the 1970s and 1980s. Other contributors to the battle are often treated as a sidelight to the clash of heavy armor. We contend that as battlefield information systems and modern munitions become increasingly effective, and as we confront situations where few armored forces are available to defend friendly territory in the early stages of a conflict, models that embody these traditional approaches to warfare will become less and less useful for assessing future capabilities.

A Simpler Approach to Assessing Modern Firepower

Like many elements of the theater-level models, our approach contains a number of simplifying assumptions. However, our approach has the virtue of transparency: The process by which inputs are turned into outputs can be readily grasped, and all of our assumptions are open to inspection. Hence, the reader can decide which, if any, variables should be changed. And it is easy to evaluate the effects of such changes. The model is embedded in an automated spreadsheet, so that it takes only a few minutes to set up and run a new variation of any case. Thus, it is possible to examine numerous "what ifs" around any particular scenario.

Our approach starts with a moving, mechanized enemy ground force that we assume is confined to a discrete number of main axes of advance (see Figure 4.3). The number of axes can be varied from run to run. We assume in our base case that the lead elements of enemy forces moving along each axis travel at an average rate of 70 kilometers per day unless they encounter significant resistance in the form of either an opposing ground force or heavy and effective firepower. (For the sake of clarity and because friendly armored forces are few in number in these cases, we attempt to account for kills achieved only by firepower from friendly aircraft and missiles.) As U.S. and al-

RAND*MR958-4.3*

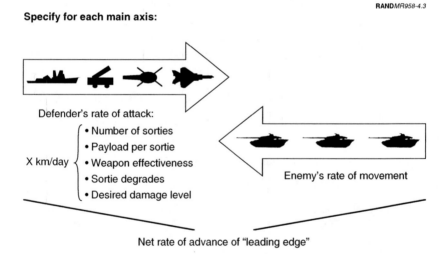

Figure 4.3—Estimating FEBA Movement: A Simple Model

lied forces attack each element of the advancing force to a specified high level of damage, we assume that those units are pulled out of the line of march for the remainder of the halt phase.[8] The net advance of the leading edge of the unattacked units on any given day is then the difference between the "base rate" (in this case, 70 kilometers) and the column length (in kilometers) that can be attacked with sufficient lethality to achieve the damage level necessary to render the attacking units ineffective.[9]

The number of kilometers' worth of columns attacked each day is determined by those factors contributing to the amount and effectiveness of longer-range antiarmor firepower: the number of assets available, their sortie rate, their payload and weapon characteristics, the portion of attack assets that actually find valid targets (determined by the surveillance, assessment, and battle management assets available), and the level of damage that is deemed necessary to compel an enemy unit to cease its advance.

The overall "flow" of the model, along with typical values assumed for each variable on Day X of our base-case run, is shown in Figure 4.4. The figure shows, for example, that the 50 B-1B aircraft in-theater on that day had a sortie rate of .75. Hence, the aircraft were assumed to fly a total of 37 sorties per day, all of which were allocated to attacking moving armored columns. Of these sorties, 21 are assumed to have attacked their intended targets (that is, enemy armor). Those sorties delivered a total of 750 WCMDs, each filled with 40 Skeet—smart antiarmor submunitions. In a similar way, the other appropriate firepower assets—fixed-wing fighter bombers, attack helicopters, and ATACMS missiles—are allocated to destroy and halt moving armor.

---

[8]A certain portion of the armored vehicles destroyed each day—normally around 10 percent in our analysis—is assumed to be immediately repaired and returned to the line of march.

[9]This approach—halting at the individual unit level and estimating the net rate of advance of the leading edge of enemy units—is distinct from standard methods applied in most theater models. These models assume, in effect, that movement of ground forces without ground opposition continues unabated until their *overall* level of losses reaches a certain threshold. Such an approach fails to take full account of effects that attacks on columns near the leading edge of the attacking force would have on that force's rate of advance.

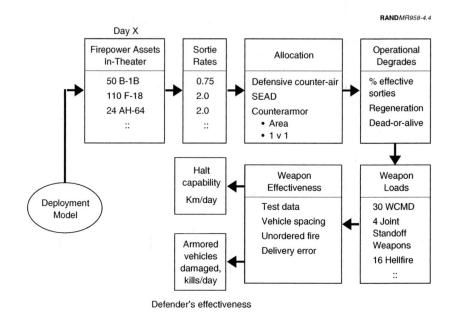

Figure 4.4—A Transparent Approach to Assessing the Halt Force

Why did fewer than two-thirds of the sorties find and engage valid targets—columns of undamaged enemy armored vehicles?[10] Because we take account only of those assets that engage and damage armor, assets that attack anything else are seen as either supporting the armor "killers" or wasted. These "wasted" attacks—

_____

[10]We use armor kills and kilometers of column effectively damaged as our chief measures of effectiveness because the number of tanks, armored fighting vehicles, armored personnel carriers, and self-propelled artillery—the "big four"—is the measure of a ground force's combat potential that is most widely used in the U.S. defense community. We recognize that there is great value in destroying the "soft-skinned" trucks that carry personnel, spare parts, consumables, and other cargo vital to the prosecution of a fast-moving land campaign. Likewise, the defender can impose significant delays on the attacker by dropping bridges, interdicting rail lines, and otherwise disrupting key transportation nodes. But because the connections between damage to these support assets and a force's immediate combat capabilities are difficult to quantify, we do not attempt to capture these effects in our analysis. (Like most other assumptions made herein, this grounds the analysis on the conservative side from the standpoint of the defender.)

allocated to the attack of armor but failing to engage valid armor targets—may arise for a variety of reasons. Terminal area defenses may prevent an effective engagement. Camouflage, concealment, or deception measures may allow an armored unit to avoid detection. Weapons may be employed to attack a column that has already been effectively damaged by other assets. Or columns of trucks and other soft-skinned vehicles might be mistaken for armored vehicles and attacked. The last problem can be particularly vexing: Because the overall battlefield will nearly always contain many more soft-skinned vehicles than armor, there is a high premium on assets that can quickly and reliably locate the armor and help direct attack assets to the most lucrative clusters of targets.

We assume that by the middle part of the next decade—the time frame of this study—assets such as JSTARS, UAVs, and other sensor platforms will provide sufficient data to assessment centers to allow them to locate columns of moving vehicles, a high portion of them armored, even when the columns are interspersed among a host of unarmored vehicles. Specifically, we assume that during the halt phase, when large numbers of armored vehicles are moving, more than one-third of the sorties allocated to the attack of moving armor fail to find and engage columns rich in armored vehicles. By historical standards, this represents a high level of efficiency. However, we believe this to be a conservative assumption for U.S. force planners today in light of new capabilities of defense suppression, surveillance, and control systems.[11]

We also assume in our analysis that all U.S. sorties that attack moving armor in the opening phase of the conflict will deliver a quality antiarmor munition: most USAF aircraft deliver the WCMD/SFW, Navy and Marine aircraft deliver Joint Standoff Weapons (JSOW) with

---

[11]Of course, considerable uncertainties surround this assumption, as we have little experience with large-scale operations in the presence of advanced surveillance, assessment, and control capabilities. Certainly lower levels of efficiency are conceivable, particularly if the enemy is able to threaten or destroy key surveillance platforms, such as JSTARS. On the other hand, our limited experience with the prototype JSTARS aircraft in Operation Desert Storm and in Bosnia suggests that finding and attacking large formations of moving vehicles in types of terrain favorable to armored warfare should not be difficult. For a description of JSTARS' performance in Desert Storm, see Price Bingham, *The Battle of Al Khafji and the Future of Surveillance Precision Strike*, Aerospace Education Foundation, Arlington, VA, 1997.

SFW, attack helicopters deliver Hellfire missiles, and ATACMS missiles deliver BAT. Thus, we may "expend" larger numbers of such weapons than are currently programmed. We return to this issue below, but for now we note that attacking assets in the opening phase of a conflict with anything less than the best available munitions would understate, by a wide margin, the halting potential of the force. It would also represent a poor use of resources.

Weapons and Sortie Effectiveness

For area weapons, munitions effectiveness devolves to estimating the number of weapons that must be delivered against a column of vehicles to achieve a desired level of damage. Once the average spacing between armored vehicles is specified, damage expectancy (DE) can be translated into the average number of armored vehicles damaged or destroyed per weapon expended and per sortie.

Estimating the number of weapons required encompasses a wide range of variables regarding the capabilities and limitations of the weapons themselves, U.S. operational concepts for engaging targets and delivering the weapons, and the enemy's tactics and operations. Regarding weapons, our focus is on the CBU-97/Sensor Fuzed Weapon, which incorporates the Skeet submunition, a well-tested but as yet not widely understood antiarmor weapon now in production for the United States Air Force. Figure 4.5 illustrates key components of the sensor fuzed weapon. When the dispenser released from an aircraft reaches the appropriate altitude (a few hundred feet above the ground), it opens and releases ten BLU-108 submunitions. These are slowed by parachutes, and as they approach ground level, a small rocket motor fires at the base of each munition, raising it up and spinning it. Each of the BLU-108s then tosses four Skeets along predetermined patterns. Collectively, these 40 Skeets cover an area roughly 400 meters long by 200 meters wide while in flight. Each Skeet seeks out infrared signatures characteristic of vehicles with warm engines and, if it finds one, fires at it with an explosively forged projectile (EFP) that is able to penetrate several inches of armor plate.

In more than 100 tests of CBU-97s, each weapon, or dispenser, delivered against a representative column of armored vehicles and trucks has damaged, on average, three to four armored vehicles. Average

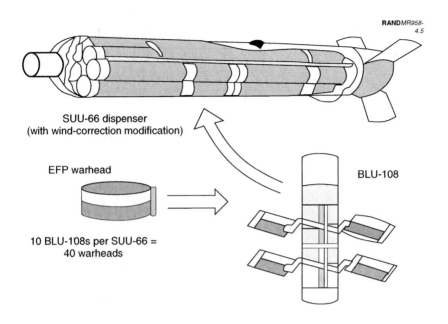

RAND*MR958-4.5*

SUU-66 dispenser
(with wind-correction modification)

EFP warhead

BLU-108

10 BLU-108s per SUU-66 =
40 warheads

Figure 4.5—The CBU-97 Antiarmor Weapon

spacing between the armored vehicles in these columns has been around 50 meters. Thus, for the eight armored vehicles that fall within a single weapon's 400-meter "footprint," we can expect that nearly half of them will be damaged to at least an "availability kill" (or "A-kill") level. This means that some component of the vehicle has been damaged to the extent that the vehicle must be withdrawn from the line of march and repaired before continuing on.[12] To make prudent assumptions about this weapon's performance under conditions of combat, we make several further assumptions. We first assume that the pattern of submunitions will not be optimally ori-

_____

[12]The "availability kill" (or "A-kill") criterion was developed as the best means of assessing the value of attacks on vehicles in second-echelon formations; that is, units that are hours or days from reaching contact with friendly ground forces. In such cases, the more widely used mobility kill (M-kill) or firepower kill (F-kill) criteria, which are applied to vehicles that are disabled within 15 minutes of an attack, are too severe and would fail to capture the value of attacks that inflict somewhat less damage but still accomplish the objective of removing a vehicle from the line of march, at least temporarily.

ented vis-à-vis the segment of road being attacked. In the heat of combat, not every aircrew will be able to orient their weapons ideally, particularly as most of the time these weapons will be delivered in "sticks" of four or more at a time.[13] In light of this, we assume that instead of each weapon covering a 400-meter-long segment of column, only about 270 meters would be covered.

We next estimate the effects when multiple weapons are delivered against a column. We know that we must expect diminishing returns to scale as bomblets are delivered with increasing density. Again, a range of outcomes is possible. At one end of the spectrum, the weapons could be delivered with optimal spacing, such that each pattern just overlapped its neighbors, providing "double" coverage over the entire segment of road attacked. In Figure 4.6, we refer to this approach as "ordered fire." For a situation in which each pattern measured 270 meters in length, it would take seven weapons to cover one kilometer of road in this fashion. This density of bomblets would damage more than 70 percent of the armored vehicles within the weapon's footprint. We judge that this level of damage would be sufficient to render a unit at least temporarily incapable of continued effective operations—the unit can be considered to have halted for the time being.

At the other end of the spectrum, the weapons could be delivered randomly within the segment of column attacked. We refer to this as "unordered fire." Here, some sections of column are triple covered or more, while others are totally uncovered. In this case, ten weapons would be required per kilometer to achieve the same level of damage expectancy (>70 percent) as the seven optimally laid down weapons. (For a more detailed explication of our calculations regarding munitions effectiveness, see the appendix.) Guided dispensers, such as the WCMD and JSOW, should allow a result closer tothe optimal. Nevertheless, to be confident that we are not overstating the effectiveness of future antiarmor capabilities, we assume less-efficient random deliveries.

---

[13]The WCMD and the JSOW both incorporate an inertial guidance unit that permits them to be dropped on a particular aimpoint with considerable accuracy (around 30 meters). However, because these remain developmental weapons at the time of this writing and tactics for their delivery have not yet been developed, we have made a conservative assumption about their alignment with target arrays.

RAND*MR958-4.6*

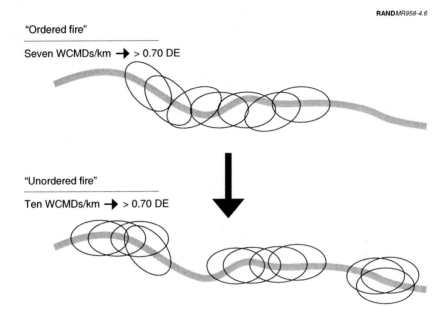

**Figure 4.6—Estimating Skeet's Effectiveness: Optimal Versus
Random Deliveries**

Hence, in most of the cases that follow, we allot ten WCMD or ten
JSOW for each kilometer segment of armored column attacked.
Again, with this density of submunitions, we conclude that at least 70
percent of the armored vehicles within every kilometer segment of
column attacked are damaged to the extent that they would require
repair.

Figure 4.7 summarizes the net effect of these assumptions with respect to sortie effectiveness. A single F-16 can carry four CBU-97
weapons. If those weapons together were each as effective as the
single weapons delivered in tests (that is, if we realized linear returns
to scale), we would expect that each F-16 sortie would be able to hit
more than 12 to 13 armored vehicles, and that it would damage most
of these. Note that this estimate is extrapolated from tests in which
the armored vehicles were separated by an average of 50 meters.
Intervehicular spacing of as much as 50 meters would be characteristic of a highly disciplined force, particularly once heavy attacks

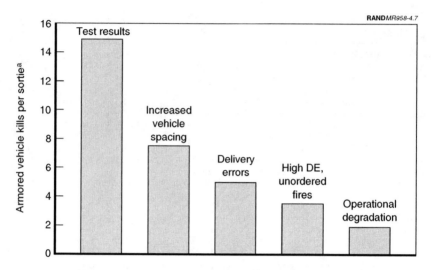

**Figure 4.7—Assumptions Regarding Sortie Effectiveness: Skeet
Antiarmor Munitions**

began. Nevertheless, we degrade that level of effectiveness first by
assuming that the enemy can maintain, *on average,* 100 meters
between each armored vehicle on the march. (The space between
armored vehicles could be occupied by trucks or other soft-skinned
vehicles.) This assumption allows us to account for the possibility
that coalition antiarmor sorties will encounter some armored
formations with spacing considerably greater than 100 meters. For
example, a unit that expected to encounter opposition in its line of
march might disperse off the road into a tactical formation in which
the average distance between its combat vehicles was around 200
meters or more. In effect, we assume that advanced surveillance,
assessment, and control capabilities will allow longer-range
firepower assets to locate and engage enemy armored formations
that are as lucrative as the average across the theater.

As Figure 4.7 shows, we next assume the delivery errors outlined
above. We also account for the diminishing returns to scale and
operational degrades mentioned earlier. The net effect of these

assumptions is to reduce our estimate of expected armored vehicle kills for a typical sortie by almost 90 percent from levels demonstrated in tests. This seems prudent, if not pessimistic.

Enemy forces that are aware they may be attacked by weapons such as Skeet can take steps to reduce their vulnerability. Some possible countermeasures—most notably, increased spacing between vehicles and efforts to confuse U.S. sensors about the location of tanks and other armored vehicles—have already been factored into our baseline assessment of munitions effectiveness. But other countermeasures are possible. For example, enemy forces could attempt to disperse laterally by using secondary roads or by moving off-road—a case we examine below. Enemy ground forces might also use camouflage and concealment, smoke, or other measures to suppress their vehicles' visual and infrared (IR) signatures. The enemy might add more armor plate or reactive armor to vulnerable areas on the tops of their vehicles. Or enemy forces might concentrate their movement over the span of a few hours per day, seeking shelter in favorable terrain at other times. If the movements of an entire invasion force could be coordinated in this way, it might substantially reduce the number of opportunities that antiarmor assets would have to attack the force.

None of these measures is likely to be truly effective, however. By focusing attacks on moving vehicles, we limit the amount of camouflage that the enemy can employ. Explosive reactive armor is intended to deflect antiarmor munitions that fuze on impact, but Skeet's explosively forged projectile is formed at some distance from the target and is traveling at great speed (several thousand feet per second) when it arrives. Although more testing may be called for, reactive armor would not seem to be a promising counter to Skeet.

By coordinating and "pulsing" movement times, enemy forces could reduce periods of vulnerability, but at a price: To move large forces efficiently in a short time will require more tightly spaced columns of vehicles, increasing the vulnerability of forces when they are on the move. Moreover, enemy forces in assembly areas will not generally be immune from attack, especially in open terrain.

Finally, an enhanced version of Skeet is now in development and should be operational by the turn of the century. This preplanned product improvement (P3I) version of the warhead will incorporate an active sensor that can detect the profile of potential targets acquired by the IR sensors. This detection will permit greater sensitivity in the IR sensors, making it more difficult both to obscure sources of IR energy and to spoof the munition into firing at heat sources not associated with vehicles. We have not adjusted our estimates of sortie effectiveness to account for either of these more exotic potential countermeasures or the enhanced performance of the P3I warhead. Preliminary tests and analyses suggest that the new weapon will be substantially more effective than the existing one: Only 60 percent as many P3I weapons will need to be delivered to achieve the same damage expectancy under comparable conditions.[14]

In summary, there are many possible countermeasures to what we are describing. Many have been incorporated into this analysis, and promising counter-countermeasures are in development for others. On balance, it appears likely that smart antiarmor munitions will maintain their effectiveness into the future.

RESULTS OF THE BASE CASE

Figure 4.8 shows the number of fixed- and rotary-wing sorties available over the first 12 days of our baseline scenario. (ATACMS shots are also included in counterarmor sorties.) One can clearly see the shift in emphasis from "enabling" over the first five days to direct attacks against armor after that. The key to this shift is degrading the enemy's airborne and surface-based air defenses to the point that nonstealthy aircraft, such as the B-1B, the F-15E, and other fighter-bombers, can operate with relatively low risk at medium altitudes.

Figure 4.9 tracks the enemy's ability to press the attack in the face of the counterarmor capacity of U.S. longer-range firepower assets,

---

[14]Briefings and discussions at Project "Chicken Little," the joint munitions test and evaluation program at Eglin Air Force Base, FL.

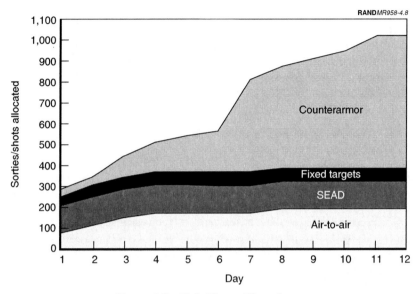

Figure 4.8—Halt Phase Allocations

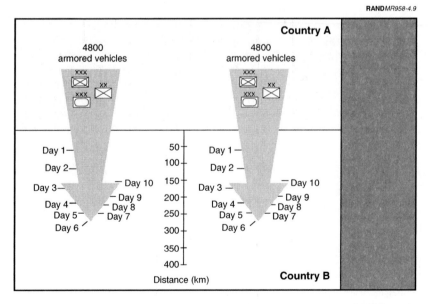

**Figure 4.9—Net Advance of Unattacked Enemy Forces Along
Two Main Axes**

assuming that all of the counterarmor assets deliver a quality munition. Again, we have assumed a "base" velocity of 70 kilometers per
day along two main axes. At first, while U.S. forces are few in number
and preoccupied with enabling efforts, enemy forces make good
progress. By Day 6 of the campaign, however, U.S. firepower has
been able to reach and, by Day 7, to exceed the capacity to attack 140
kilometers of armored column daily; that is, 70 kilometers along each
of two main axes of advance. This has the effect of halting and then
pushing back the point of advance of the enemy's unattacked ground
forces. The furthest point reached by columns of vehicles before
they have been attacked—the enemy ground force's "high water
mark"—is approximately 260 kilometers beyond the prewar
boundary. After that, enemy columns are halted short of this point.
By Day 10, U.S. firepower assets have attacked and heavily damaged
every armored column that enemy ground forces can generate, even
if the enemy chooses to put every armored unit committed to the
offensive on the move.

Figure 4.10 summarizes these results and introduces the format that
is used throughout this report to present the results of each case.
The figure shows, for each day of the halt campaign, the furthest
point of advance for the enemy's unattacked units, plotted in
kilometers against the scale on the left. The figure also shows the
cumulative number of enemy armored vehicles damaged or destroyed, plotted against the right-hand axis. Here, we estimate that
U.S. firepower assets could damage more than 7000 armored vehicles
out of a total of 9600 committed to the attack, assuming they are all
put on the move.[15]

Once every armored unit on the move has been attacked to the damage expectancy goal of at least 70 percent, we assume that the
enemy's attack has been, for all intents and purposes, halted. Note
that this occurs on Day 10, at which point the rate of kill drops
dramatically. U.S. forces find it more difficult to locate undamaged

---

[15]Note that this assessment does not account for enemy armored vehicles that might
be damaged or destroyed by indigenous allied air and ground forces. It is assumed
that the number of such kills will be modest in this type of short-warning scenario.
Hence, for simplicity and to assess a limiting, stressful case, we take account of kills by
U.S. forces only.

RAND*MR958-4.10*

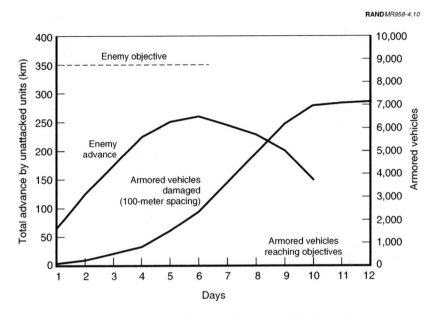

**Figure 4.10—Enemy Advance and Armor Kills: Base Case,
Unlimited Weapons**

enemy armored vehicles once they halt, because the enemy can begin to find or create cover and concealment for his vehicles and because surveillance assets and crews of attacking aircraft are apt to have some difficulty in distinguishing unattacked vehicles from those that have been damaged. At this point, U.S. fixed-wing assets cease expending area munitions and shift to attacks with "one-on-one" weapons, such as the AGM-86 Maverick missile and laser-guided bombs, which are targeted against individual vehicles rather than moving columns.

Figure 4.10 shows our estimate of the number of enemy armored vehicles that reach their objective, defined in this scenario as being a line 350 kilometers from the prewar border.[16] Obviously, in this case, the estimate is that no vehicles reach this point.

---

[16]Our choice of 350 kilometers is not entirely arbitrary: It is less distance than Iraqi forces would have to travel to reach Dhahran or Chinese forces to reach Seoul. It is somewhat further than forces from Belarus would have to travel to Warsaw in a hypothetical invasion of Poland.

It is worth examining which systems contributed to the successful halt achieved in this scenario. Figure 4.11 shows total numbers of armored vehicles damaged by platform type and, at the top of each bar, the average number of armored vehicles destroyed per sortie. (These figures include "wasted" sorties given imperfections in U.S. battlefield surveillance, assessment, control functions, and other operational factors.)

Overall, Figure 4.11 highlights the importance of quickly deploying fixed-wing aircraft. Given a fairly modest-sized joint force deployed forward in peacetime and an enemy attack prior to reinforcement, this finding may seem obvious. But only recently have fighter-bombers and, especially, bombers begun to acquire weapons and engagement systems that allow them to be this effective in an antiarmor role.

Perhaps the most striking conclusion that emerges from this figure is the potential of large payload aircraft, such as the B-1B, to damage moving armor. With approximately 2400 kills, the 50 B-1B aircraft

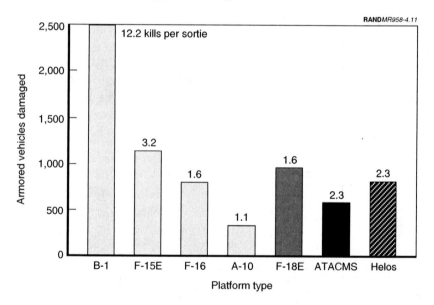

Figure 4.11—Kills Against Moving Armor by Platform Type: Base Case, Unlimited Weapons

deployed in our scenario accounted for more than one-third of the entire joint force's armor kills during the halt phase. This level of effectiveness results from the B-1's large payload and the availability of a highly capable antiarmor weapon that can be delivered from medium altitude. Within the time frame of this analysis, the B-1B is programmed to carry and deliver 30 WCMDs in a single sortie.[17] This carriage capacity together with the aircraft's long range, which allows it to be based beyond the strike capabilities of most regional adversaries, makes the modified B-1 a highly attractive asset in the halt phase. By the same token, the F-15E, which can carry at least twice as much ordnance as most other fighter-bombers, also plays a disproportionately large role in halting the attack. (The absolute numbers of kills shown here, which are probably on the low side for all platforms, are less important than the relative kills per sortie.)

The ATACMS missile, whether launched from ground-based MLRS vehicles or perhaps eventually from ships, can play an important role as well. If the missiles and their launchers are deployed forward in advance of the conflict and if the advanced BAT munition proves to be effective, this system can be employed in the opening days of the halt campaign even before the enemy's air defenses have been suppressed. The ATACMS missile thus denies the enemy ground force a "free ride" even during the portion of the campaign that is most stressful for the defender.

Finally, note that nearly 9000 WCMD and 2000 JSOW, both filled with Skeet submunitions, were expended in this case. (It was assumed that most USAF aircraft employed WCMD, while Navy and Marine aircraft employed JSOW.) These numbers compare to currently programmed inventories for these weapons of around 5000 WCMD/Skeet and 3000 JSOW/Skeet by the Air Force, and fewer than 1500 JSOW/Skeet by the Navy and Marines.[18] The programmed force can

---

[17]This assumes that all three of the B-1's bomb bays are filled with weapons, a configuration that would permit the aircraft a combat radius of approximately 1750 nautical miles and might necessitate an in-flight refueling in some scenarios. Other upgrades to the B-1 needed to permit accurate delivery of WCMD include upgrading each bomb bay and rack to MILSTD 1760, allowing Global Positioning System (GPS) and inertial coordinate data to be passed to each weapon, and improving weapon station instrumentation to allow for aimpoint designation.

[18]Figures are approximate and reflect planned inventories circa 2005.

probably prevail in scenarios that offer lengthy periods of buildup prior to the commencement of hostilities, because sufficient attack assets would be deployed to permit a brute force approach of destroying armor with large numbers of these and other less-capable munitions. But a robust power projection capability in the face of a determined adversary and a stressing, short-warning scenario would demand munitions that get the most lethality possible out of every sortie.

Variations of the Base Case: Multiple Axes of Advance and Increased Spacing

Having presented this base case, we now briefly examine a series of possible alternative cases. Perhaps the most obvious of these is one in which enemy ground forces are able to advance along more than two main axes. This case could pertain either to theaters where the terrain is flat, firm, and open, permitting off-road movement at least by tracked vehicles; or to theaters where a dense road network allows both tracked and wheeled vehicles to move forward in parallel along many different routes. We summarize the outcome of such a case in Figure 4.12. Here, we assume that enemy ground forces move along seven distinct avenues of advance. However, because some avenues are assumed to have less capacity than the two main axes in our base case, the average movement rate for columns decreases from 70 kilometers per day to 40. We keep constant all of the other variables from the base case.[19]

Under these conditions, enemy forces are worse off than in the base case: They lose approximately the same number of armored vehicles (around 7200), but they reach their "high water mark" at only 240 kilometers beyond the prewar boundary (versus 260 in the base

---

[19]More than seven axes are, of course, possible. In the limit, the armored vehicles of a large mechanized force could spread out, off of roads, in tactical formations tens or hundreds of kilometers in width. But it would be impractical for a force to transit hundreds of kilometers in this fashion, even if the terrain were favorable. Hence, we assume that for some portion of its advance the attacking force is confined to roads. Even in Central Europe, where the transportation infrastructure is fairly well developed, studies of Soviet and NATO ground forces' movement options during the Cold War concluded that these forces would quickly saturate the road networks, imposing strict trade-offs between transit speeds and vehicle spacing (and, hence, vulnerability to area weapons). See Simpkin, 1985, pp. 44, 80, and 299.

RAND*MR958-4.12*

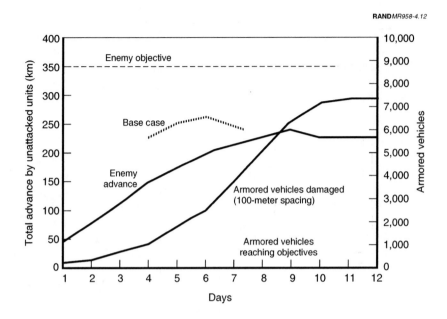

**Figure 4.12—Enemy Advance and Armor Kills: Multiple
Axes of Advance, Slowed Movement**

case). By moving along more axes, enemy forces can quickly generate more of columns that must be neutralized each day to halt the
attack. But this effect is more than compensated for by the reduced
speed of movement, particularly in the early days of the conflict,
when U.S. forces are few in number and preoccupied with gaining
freedom of action. Given that secondary roads or off-road routes will
always have less capacity than major roads, and given the added
complexity of coordinating the movement of a large mechanized
force along multiple axes, some trade-off between the number of
axes and average velocity seems inescapable.[20]

Another obvious counter to area antiarmor weapons, such as Skeet,
is to reduce target density. That is, the enemy could spread out the

---

[20]Determining the exact nature of this trade-off in any specific case would require
detailed terrain and trafficability analyses that are beyond the scope of this study and
its generic scenario.

armored vehicles more widely so that each weapon delivered engaged fewer targets. Figure 4.13 shows one such case. It is assumed that the average spacing between armored vehicles on the move is 200 meters rather than 100. The number of axes (seven) and the average velocity (40 km per day) remain the same as in the previous case.

Here we see that enemy ground forces are again confronted with a dilemma: By extending the spacing between armored vehicles, the enemy has indeed decreased its vulnerability to individual attacks by most of the area weapons. As one would expect, this reduces both the number of armored vehicles damaged and the rate of damage in the opening days of the war. But the enemy has paid a price as well. By opening up the distance between armored vehicles, it has reduced the number of armored vehicles that can occupy any particular avenue of advance at any one time. This has several effects:

RAND*MR958-4.13*

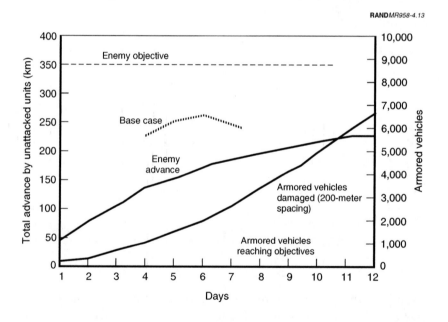

Figure 4.13—Enemy Advance and Armor Kills: Multiple Axes of Advance, Slowed Movement, Increased Spacing

- The overall transit time for the force is increased.

- The capability of limited area weapons, such as the sensor fuzed weapon, to maintain a given damage expectancy over a kilometer of enemy column ("halt potential," as we have defined it) is unaffected. The number of vehicles damaged by such attacks is, however, reduced.

- The halt potential of one-on-one weapons (such as Maverick or Hellfire) or broad area weapons (such as BAT) is *increased*. For such weapons, vehicle kills are unaffected by spacing, and the number of vehicles per kilometer of column is reduced.

The net result is similar to the 100-meter spacing case—a penetration of about 240 kilometers into friendly territory and around 6700 armored vehicles damaged, with halt imminent on Day 13. This case illustrates an important point: when faced with a mix of U.S. weapons, the opposing commander has no simple options for vehicle spacing. Tighter spacing may improve the speed at which the force can be massed, but will dramatically increase the vulnerability of the armor of area weapons like Skeet. Wider spacing both slows the force and actually improves the halt potential of one-on-one weapons. This result highlights the importance of a mix of weapons and joint forces, and is discussed at greater length in the appendix.

Note that later-arriving firepower assets play a larger role in this case, as the number of armored vehicles damaged in the very early days is reduced. Also noteworthy is that a substantially higher number of air-delivered antiarmor weapons are needed in order to enforce the halt in this case (17,000 Skeet-dispensing weapons, as opposed to fewer than 11,000 in the base case). Whereas kills by ATACMS/BAT, helicopters, and A-10s are not measurably affected by the reduced density of targets, fixed-wing aircraft delivering Skeet submunitions are damaging only half as many armored vehicles per sortie. Even at this increased spacing, this weapon remains by far the best armor killer available for high-payload aircraft such as the B-1B and F-15E, but larger quantities of area antiarmor munitions would be needed if greatly increased spacing is regarded as a tactically viable countermeasure by the enemy.

Confronting the Threat of Weapons of Mass Destruction

We noted earlier that U.S. adversaries would like to be able to achieve their objectives without incurring the enormous risks and uncertainties associated with the use of weapons of mass destruction—nuclear weapons and lethal chemical or biological agents. However, such use cannot be ruled out in the halt phase, particularly if the United States and its allies present their adversaries with a posture that is manifestly capable of denying them their objectives in the absence of large-scale WMD use. How might future joint commanders react to such threats, and what might their effects be on the halt campaign?[21]

First, the threat of WMD use can be expected to affect the ways in which outside forces deploy to the theater. At a minimum, U.S. leaders would want to minimize the number of assets and personnel within range of the most numerous enemy delivery means. Figure 4.14 illustrates what this might mean in the Gulf region. The figure shows the area that Iraq could cover with the 450-kilometer-range Scud-C missile. In assessing the potential effectiveness of such a capability, we assume here that no fixed-wing, land-based U.S. aircraft are deployed to bases within 500 kilometers of enemy territory. Of course, this does not render these forces immune from attacks with WMD—over time, U.S. adversaries can be expected to develop or to procure delivery vehicles with ranges greater than the Scud-C. But given the expense of these longer-range delivery vehicles, greater range implies that U.S. forces will be subjected to a lower rate and a smaller total number of attacking missiles. Greater range also offers battle space within which active defenses can gain multiple engagement opportunities and, hence, a higher probability of destroying attacking missiles. Space also translates into more time for attack assessment, allowing some forces to continue normal operations once impact points have been predicted.

Bases under attack will experience reductions in their tempo of operations for some period of time, as operations are interrupted in or-

---

[21]For an in-depth assessment of the problem of constraints on access by U.S. forces to the Persian Gulf region, see Paul K. Davis, William Schwabe, and Bruce Nardulli, *Mitigating Effects of Access Problems in Persian Gulf Contingencies,* RAND, MR-915-OSD, forthcoming.

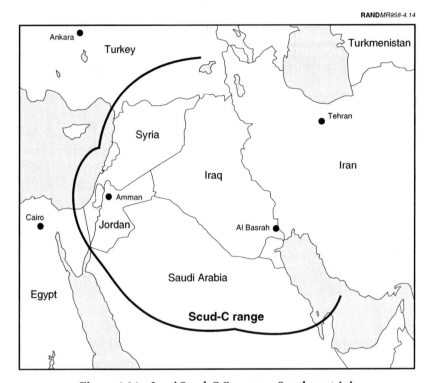

Figure 4.14—Iraqi Scud-C Coverage: Southwest Asia

der to assess the extent of each attack and as personnel are forced to work in protective suits. Estimates of the severity of reduction and the duration of the recovery period depend on a host of variables, including the type of agents used, the payload delivered, the accuracy and efficiency of the payload, the weather and time of day, and the extent and effectiveness of passive protection measures.

Table 4.2 provides our assumptions of an operations tempo degradation with respect to aircraft that participate in attacks on moving armor in the halt phase. Essentially, we assess the effects on the halt phase if WMD were able to reduce by one-half the sortie rates of all but the longest-range land-based aircraft. We also assume that carrier sorties and ATACMS availability are not affected. Because of their limited range and slow speeds, attack helicopters are not moved to the rear. They remain forward, but they move more

Table 4.2

Comparative Sortie Rates for Land-Based Forces

Aircraft	Baseline Sortie Rate	Sortie Rate with WMD
B-1B	0.75	0.5
F-15E	1.67	0.9
F-16	2.0	1.0
A-10	2.0	1.0
AH-64	2.0	1.0

frequently to reduce the probability that the enemy might locate and target them.

Figure 4.15 shows the effect of this change on our chief measures of effectiveness: enemy penetration distance and armor kills. Not sur-

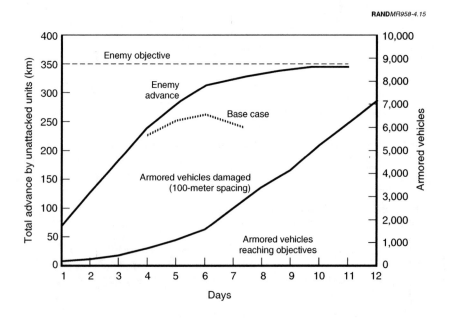

RAND*MR958-4.15*

Figure 4.15—Enemy Advance and Armor Kills: WMD, Unlimited Weapons

prisingly, we see enemy forces penetrating further than in the base case—340 kilometers as opposed to 260—and we see a drop of about 12 percent in the number of armored vehicles destroyed, or 850 fewer vehicles. The main point is that we do not see a catastrophic reduction in the effectiveness of U.S. firepower assets in the halt phase, even when the sortie rates of land-based aircraft are substantially reduced. The "halt force" remains effective, because the most capable attack platforms (B-1Bs and F-15Es) are based beyond the range of most of the enemy's missiles to begin with; because attack assets are equipped with highly capable munitions; and because, as each day passes, additional attack capacity is deployed into the theater and brought to bear against the enemy. This approach to power projection, in short, appears to be fairly robust given uncertainties about the effects of WMD use and about access to land bases in the vicinity of the enemy's advancing forces.

Exploring the Contributions of Carrier Aviation

The previous case assumed that carrier operations were not affected by enemy WMD use. Depending on the delivery systems and the surveillance assets available to the enemy, this assumption may or may not be warranted. Three more cases shed light on the sensitivity of our results to changes in carrier operations.

Delayed Access for Aircraft Carriers. In the first case, we assume that the enemy, using constricting terrain, sophisticated mines, and quiet submarines, delays access of reinforcing maritime forces to the theater for a period of two weeks or so. In this case, the carrier that is in the region at the outset of the conflict continues operations unimpeded, but the second carrier, which arrives on D+7, as in the base case, operates at only half the normal sortie rate, because it is constrained to less-favorable operating areas pending success in the antisubmarine and mine-sweeping efforts. Figure 4.16 shows that the effect of these changes on the outcome is minimal relative to the base case.

Denial of Carrier Operations. Of course, we cannot be certain that the carrier on the scene at D-day would be unaffected by enemy action. In particular, antiship missiles, such as the Exocet, Silkworm, and HY-4, may pose real threats to the operations of all types of surface vessels, including carriers. To test the robustness of the joint

RAND*MR958-4.16*

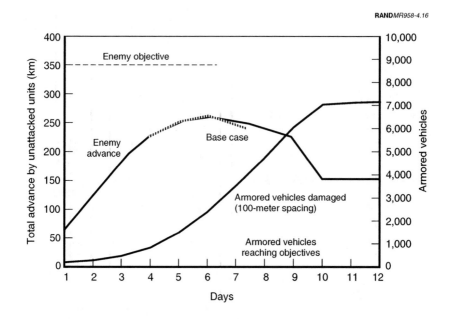

**Figure 4.16—Enemy Advance and Armor Kills: Delayed Access
for Carrier Forces**

force in the face of these threats, we examine the limiting case in
which no carrier sorties are available for the halt phase. In this case,
land-based forces must provide all of the SEAD and ground attack
sorties that the carriers provided in the base case—more enabling
forces must be deployed by air early in the conflict, and more time
passes before U.S. forces can shift their efforts to heavy attacks on
the enemy's armored formations. Table 4.3 shows the deployments
assumed for this case.

Figure 4.17 shows the results of these assumptions. In the absence of
carrier-based aviation, land-based assets require an additional two
days to provide the same number of sorties that had been available
in the base case to suppress enemy air defenses and missiles. This
need to replace carrier sorties in the enabling portion of the halt
phase results in lost sorties for attacking armor for several days. As a
result, enemy forces are able to penetrate more deeply than in the
base case, almost to their objective.

Table 4.3

Assumed Deployment: No Carrier Operations, Halt Phase

Day	Forces (Fighter aircraft in squadrons)
0 (in-place)	2 ×[a] F-15C, F-16(L), A-10, F-16 (HTS), 1 × Bn AH-64, 250 ATACMS
1	F-22, F-117, 8 B-2
2	F-22, 3 × ABL
3	F-16HTS, F-15C
4	F-15C
5	F-15C, F-16 HTS
6	F-15E, 50 B-1B
7	F-15E, 2 × F/A-18C/D
8	F-16(L)
9	F-16(L), F-15E
10	F-15E
11	F-16(L)
12	2 × F-16

[a]× = units.

RAND*MR958-4.17*

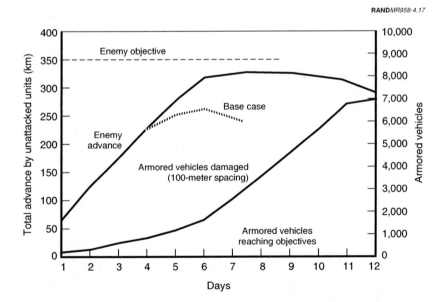

Figure 4.17—Enemy Advance and Armor Kills: No Carrier Sorties

To achieve a result at least as good as the base case (i.e., limiting enemy penetration to 260 kilometers) but without carrier participation, USAF force elements would need to be allocated roughly 100 additional tons of the daily intertheater airlift capacity—a 12 percent increase over the 900 tons per day assumed in the base case.

Massive Naval Forces Only. These cases suggest that carriers deployed routinely in areas where U.S. interests might be threatened provide valuable capabilities early in a short-warning conflict. Carrier-based air is especially useful to the extent that it can help speed the "enabling" phase of the joint campaign by suppressing and destroying enemy air defenses and high-leverage fixed targets, such as command and control centers, airfields, and key choke points along the enemy's route of advance. This utility, however, is quite distinct from the ability, claimed by some observers, of carrier-based aviation to serve as a hedge against the possibility that U.S. air forces might not gain access to theater land bases in wartime.[22]

To test the latter proposition, we present a case that eliminates USAF, Marine, and Army land-based air forces from the joint force deployed in the base case. We replace that force with a truly robust naval power projection force. Specifically, we assume that two CVBGs and three arsenal ships (each with 250 ATACMS missiles) are in the theater and within range of targets on D-day. We further assume that a third CVBG arrives on D+3 and a fourth on D+7. The first two carriers conduct an enabling operation that allows all sorties from the reinforcing carriers to be allocated to antiarmor attacks. Even if all of the antiarmor sorties from this armada were equipped with highly effective antiarmor weapons, we see in Figure 4.18 that it cannot halt a determined invasion: The enemy begins to accumulate ground forces at the objective by Day 9, and by Day 12 approximately

---

[22]Davis and Kugler, for example, endorse the Bottom-Up Review's call for five carrier battle groups (CVBGs) as part of the building block of forces appropriate for a single major regional conflict, noting that "the United States has two ways to achieve early airpower in a contingency [by deploying land-based and carrier-based air], and it should savor and preserve that flexibility." In any case, the total number of carriers is determined more by the demands of day-to-day "presence" operations than by their contributions to major theater conflicts. See Paul K. Davis and Richard L. Kugler, "New Principles for Force Sizing," in Zalmay M. Khalilzad and David A. Ochmanek (eds.), *Strategic Appraisal 1997: Strategy and Defense Planning for the 21st Century*, RAND, MR-826-AF, 1997.

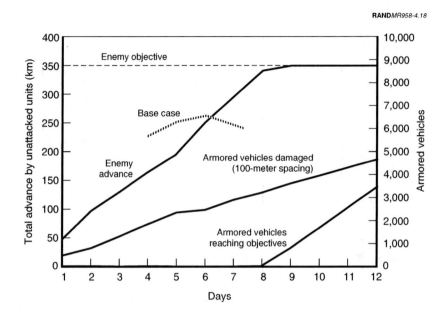

RAND*MR958-4.18*

Figure 4.18—Enemy Advance and Armor Kills: Massive Naval Force

3500 armored vehicles—the equivalent of more than four divisions—are in place.

PRELIMINARY JUDGMENTS

In summary, we find that U.S. forces, properly equipped and supported, can attrit and halt an armored invasion fairly rapidly under stressful conditions of short warning, rapid enemy movement, and suppression of U.S. deployments and operations tempo. The analysis leads to several key judgments:

- In theaters where short-warning aggression against U.S. interests is plausible, a sizable joint force stationed or deployed forward in peacetime is called for. This force should be capable of immediate employment and prepared to conduct theater surveillance, command and control, air and missile defense, defense suppression, and precision attack of ground targets.

- Rapidly deployable land-based air forces must provide the bulk of the joint force's capabilities in situations of short-warning, large-scale attacks. Without a large and capable joint and combined force posture deployed forward, and without a much larger intertheater airlift fleet, no other type of force can bring sufficient weight of effort to bear quickly enough to halt a determined foe.

- Large numbers of advanced antiarmor munitions are required to halt mechanized invasions under stressing conditions.

A MORE LIKELY OPPONENT

The analysis thus far has been based on a set of assumptions about the enemy's ground force that are, from the defender's standpoint, conservative. We have assumed that

- The enemy commits all available armored forces to the attack, regardless of the degree of attrition to units previously engaged by U.S. and allied firepower.

- Enemy ground forces maintain, on average, 100-meter spacing between armored vehicles in column formation.

- Advancing columns average 70 kilometers per day, even when under air attack.

- In their attacks on enemy columns, U.S. forces strive for a high level of damage—more than 70 percent of armored vehicles damaged to an A-kill level or better.

The reason for this conservatism is twofold. First, when defense planning is focused on future requirements, it should generally be reasonably conservative so that if key assumptions prove faulty, some margin for error exists. After all, large-scale warfare is, by definition, a matter both of life and death and of important national interests. But we have another motivation for conservatism that goes beyond this: Our work argues for a change of fairly major proportions in how U.S. defense planners and combatant commanders approach the task of halting invasions and argues, by extension, for shifts in resources toward forces and assets needed to make this new approach a reality. As always, it is incumbent upon those who propose change to convince skeptics that the new approach should be pursued, if necessary, at the expense of accepted ways of thinking. This being the case, we have taken the harder way whenever it seemed reasonably plausible to do so. The result is a set of assessments that contravenes the conventional wisdom—U.S. forces win in cases that others show us losing. But these baseline assessments might also create an inaccurate picture of the difficulty associated with halting an invading force.

For this reason, we have examined other cases using more-reasonable assumptions about what an enemy ground force might do. In the cases that follow, we assume that

- The enemy's armored vehicles will become bunched together in scattered clusters on the battlefield once heavy attacks commence against choke points along lines of advance and on the armored columns themselves. Their average spacing will decrease from 100 meters to 50 meters.

- Attacks on key choke points, and the need to clear or reconstitute heavily damaged units in the line of march, will slow the average rate of advance of the leading edge from 70 kilometers per day to 40.

- A damage level of 50 percent, rather than 70 percent, will be sufficient to compel a unit to depart from the line of march.

Together, these assumptions make it easier for U.S. forces to halt the attack. How much easier is shown on Figure 4.19. We see that by Day 4 the United States has sufficient attack assets in-theater to exceed the rate at which the enemy can push forward mechanized units along two main axes of advance. By Day 7, every element of the enemy's ground force has been attacked to a damage level of 50 percent, and the "high-water mark"—the furthest point of advance of unattacked enemy units—is at approximately 140 kilometers, as opposed to 260. Because the defender settled for a lower level of damage to each unit, fewer armored vehicles are damaged in the halt phase of this case—around 5000 as opposed to 7200. Nevertheless, it seems likely that the enemy force would be rendered ineffective as an offensive force for an extended period of time.

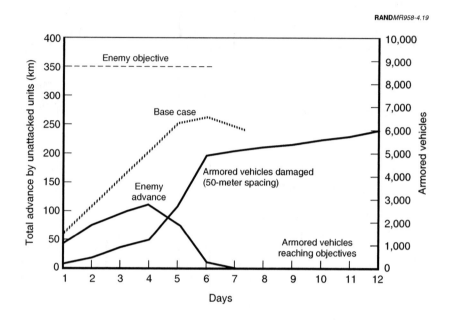

Figure 4.19—Enemy Advance and Armor Kills: Less Heroic Opponent, Base Case Forces in Place

If this case represents a more realistic appraisal of what the ground forces of a regional adversary might be able to do in the face of future U.S. opposition, it would be interesting to compare the capabilities of the forces normally deployed in the Persian Gulf region against such a threat. Figure 4.20 shows our assessment of a "Southern Watch" case. Normally, the United States deploys four squadrons of land-based fighters to the region, along with modest numbers of tankers, Airborne Warning and Control System (AWACS), and other support aircraft. No U.S. attack helicopters or BAT-equipped ATACMS missiles are routinely deployed in-theater today. More than half the time a CVBG is present in or near the Gulf. But here we assume that the first carrier arrives at D+5. Likewise, battalion-sized units are often exercising on equipment prepositioned in Kuwait, but we assume (as in the base case) that no significant Army or Marine Corps forces are present at the commencement of combat.

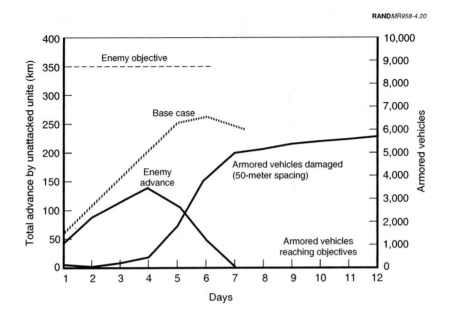

RAND*MR958-4.20*

**Figure 4.20—Enemy Advance and Armor Kills: Less Heroic Opponent,
Southern Watch Posture**

The results shown in Figure 4.20 suggest that the U.S. peacetime posture in the Gulf is probably adequate as the vanguard element of a force posture designed to defend vital economic assets in Saudi Arabia, *only if* reinforcing forces have ready access to bases on the Saudi peninsula and if adequate numbers of capable antiarmor munitions are procured and deployed forward. But this posture must be judged incapable of defending Kuwait against a surprise attack by large-scale Iraqi forces. A more robust forward posture that includes more firepower assets and some U.S. heavy ground forces would be required before we could be confident in our ability to defeat a large-scale, short-warning armored invasion short of Kuwait City and Kuwait's southern oil fields.[23]

---

[23]Current forces, rapidly reinforced, might well be capable of defeating Iraqi forces in the more likely contingency of a short-warning attack by a corps-sized or smaller Iraqi force.

CONCLUSION: LONG-RANGE FIREPOWER CAN RAPIDLY ATTRIT MECHANIZED FORCES

The analyses summarized above point to our conclusion: *Modern, longer-range firepower systems, properly supported with timely information and battle management capabilities and equipped with advanced antiarmor munitions, can effectively engage and heavily damage mechanized forces moving in large numbers.* In operational terms, this means that in theaters that do not feature heavily foliated or urbanized terrain, joint U.S. forces can rapidly halt armored invasions even in stressing scenarios, provided that sufficient investments are made in emerging concepts and systems.

The significance of this finding is magnified when our results are compared with those derived by standard DoD assessments of programmed forces. That comparison is laid out in Figure 4.21. The shaded area (labeled "Enhanced forces") shows the rate at which joint forces damage enemy armored vehicles across the range of cases discussed here. The bottom line shows a DoD assessment of the programmed force in a similar scenario. DoD's assessment

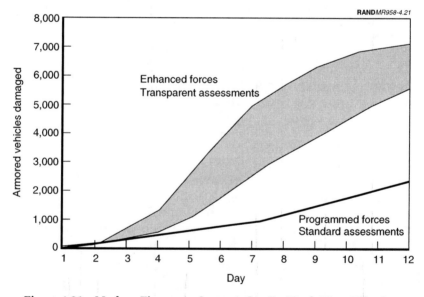

Figure 4.21—Modern Firepower Systems Can Be Much More Effective in the Halt Phase

shows the joint force damaging about 2400 armored vehicles in 12 days, compared with between 5500 and 7200 in our assessment.[24] Two factors account for most of this difference:

- First, the DoD assessment is constrained to an examination of the programmed force, meaning that far fewer advanced antiarmor munitions were available to the defender than in our cases, reducing sortie effectiveness substantially.

- Equally important, DoD's assessment is based on the output of its TACWAR model, which has grossly understated the capabilities of modern airpower and indirect fire systems.[25] By employing suboptimal mixed loads of munitions, by allocating numerous air-to-ground sorties to less lucrative sectors of the battlefield, by applying unrealistic "scalar factor" degradations to sortie effectiveness, and by other means, the model as used in the joint community systematically understates the effects of modern firepower against maneuver forces.

As a result, DoD analyses may present an erroneous picture of the overall capabilities of joint U.S. forces and, in particular, the capabilities of those forces that will play the greatest role in halting short-warning invasions: early arriving air forces.

Chapter Five discusses the implications of the above analyses for U.S. military investment priorities.

---

[24]Data on DoD's assessment of programmed forces are derived from discussions with analysts in service and joint staffs involved in recent DoD force structure studies. Different assumptions on damage criteria, enemy force spacing, sortie rates, and enemy break points account for the range between the low and high estimates of vehicles damaged in our assessments. The lower part of the range is associated with cases in which (1) mobility, firepower, and catastrophic kills are required (DoD assessments generally use these more stringent criteria), and/or (2) the opponent spaces armored vehicles 200 meters apart, and/or (3) land-based aircraft have reduced sortie rates, and/or (4) the opponent's units stop their advance at lower damage levels.

[25]As an example, in 1996 the Office of the Secretary of Defense (OSD) asked RAND to assess the capabilities of future U.S. forces in scenarios being used as part of DoD's Deep Attack Weapons Mix Study (DAWMS). The analysis team used the spreadsheet-based START model developed at RAND to conduct the analysis. Before the team was permitted to proceed, they were asked to "calibrate" START's major outputs to those of TACWAR. To get the two models to provide the same results in the same scenarios, the effectiveness of airpower in START had to be "dialed down" by 50 to 75 percent. The effectiveness of artillery had to be reduced by 95 percent.

PRIORITIES FOR MODERNIZATION: ENSURING A ROBUST CAPABILITY TO HALT INVASIONS

The preceding chapters have sketched an approach to power projection operations that offers the promise of defeating armored invasions even in highly stressing scenarios where only modest defensive forces are available in the theater at the outset of the campaign. This chapter discusses the key components of the new approach and which of them may be at risk of receiving inadequate funding.

The following capabilities are vital in gaining rapid dominance over enemy operations quickly and achieving an effective, early halt:

1. Rapid deployment and employment. In addition to maintaining a modestly sized but potent force in the theater on a routine basis, the United States requires assets to ensure that forces essential to the halt campaign can arrive in the theater within days and conduct high tempo operations. Strategic airlift constitutes the backbone of this early deployment capability. It should be supplemented by adequate stocks of prepositioned materiel, particularly high-quality munitions sufficient to sustain operations until either the halt is achieved or materiel begins to arrive by sea.[1] Aerial refueling aircraft will be needed in large numbers to assist in the deployment and employment of combat and support aircraft and to increase the capacity and utilization rate of the airlifters.

---

[1]Materiel should be prepositioned at multiple protected sites to minimize the risk of losing it in a preemptive attack. Intratheater airlift and ground transportation can distribute materiel to units.

2. Enhanced capabilities to defeat weapons of mass destruction. U.S. leaders and allies must have confidence that U.S. forces can be committed to future conflicts with acceptable costs and risks. A multipronged approach will be essential to provide the high levels of effectiveness needed not only to deter but also to prevent the use of chemical, biological, and nuclear weapons against U.S. allies and forces. This calls for capabilities to locate, identify, and destroy WMD stockpiles and their delivery vehicles before they are launched; improved, multilayered active defenses against ballistic and cruise missiles; timely and accurate capabilities for launch warning and attack assessment; and a range of passive protection measures. Capabilities to bring effective firepower to bear from longer ranges will also be required.

3. Ensuring early freedom to operate. All forces in the theater must be free from the threat of enemy air attack, and air forces must be free to observe and to attack enemy targets. Rapidly seizing the initiative in the air requires a dominant fighter—one that can enforce combat against enemy fighters and bombers and enjoy a highly favorable exchange ratio. Gaining freedom of operation over enemy forces and territory also demands effective capabilities to suppress and destroy surface-based air defenses, especially the most-capable radar-guided surface-to-air missiles (SAMs).

4. Accurate and dominant knowledge of the battlefield. Allied forces can be most effective only when they know with confidence the location and disposition of enemy forces and can deny comparable knowledge to the adversary. This requires a range of sensors and platforms to acquire data about the enemy, assessment capabilities to turn these data into information, and command and control centers to use this information to direct the activities of friendly forces.

5. Lethal firepower systems in sufficient numbers. We have already seen the tremendous leverage provided by advanced antiarmor munitions: They can increase by tenfold or more the effectiveness of aircraft assigned to destroy enemy armor. In the opening phase of a conflict, when sorties are limited and time is of the essence, it is essential that sufficient numbers of such munitions be available.

The importance of many of these capabilities can be illustrated by examining the effects of a delay in the commencement of large-scale air attacks on an enemy invasion force. In our base case, such attacks began on Days 5 and 6 of the war when F-15Es and then B-1Bs began their operations. If U.S. commanders were compelled to delay the employment of these aircraft for two more days for whatever reason—delays in achieving an adequate degree of air superiority, threats to deployment bases, or insufficient airlift to deploy supporting assets—the effect on the outcome would be significant. Figure 5.1 shows our estimate of the result, assuming an "heroic" enemy. Compared with the base case, in which enemy forces penetrated as far as 260 kilometers, we see a penetration of 350 kilometers. Eventually, the joint force pushes back the leading edge and kills roughly the same number of armored vehicles, but penetration distance is, in our estimation, quite sensitive to delays in the onset of heavy air attacks.

Not surprisingly, both penetration distance and lethality are highly dependent on the number and quality of the antiarmor munitions

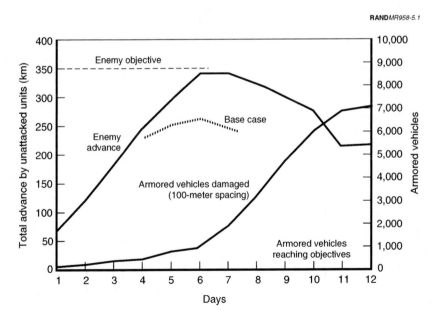

RAND*MR958-5.1*

**Figure 5.1—Enemy Advance and Armor Kills: Large-Scale Antiarmor
Attacks Delayed by Two Days**

available to the defenders. In Figure 5.2, we show the result when only 4000 Skeet dispensing weapons are available to the halt force, as opposed to the 10,500 employed in the base case. This result suggests that a highly determined adversary could capture much more ground if future U.S. air forces were compelled to fall back on older types of antiarmor munitions.

Some clear implications emerge from these results about the types of capabilities required to ensure that future U.S. forces have robust capabilities to halt a combined-arms offensive. Funding for programs to provide some of these capabilities, such as modern and capable airlift and enhanced ballistic missile defenses, does not appear to be in jeopardy. Other areas, discussed below, merit greater attention and, in some cases, greater resources. Because of the lead times associated with developing and fielding new equipment and because of the longevity of new platforms, the following points should be con-

RAND*MR958-5.2*

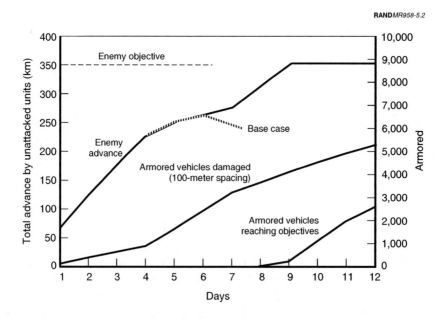

Figure 5.2—Enemy Advance and Armor Kills: Limited Stocks of
Advanced Munitions

sidered in the context of enemy capabilities that will emerge over the next ten years or more.

DEFEATING ENEMY AIRCRAFT

It is essential that U.S. and allied forces, both in place and deploying into the theater, be protected from enemy air attacks early in the conflict. At the same time, U.S. commanders will want to eliminate enemy threats to friendly offensive air operations as quickly as possible. As potential adversaries acquire more-capable fighter aircraft and, importantly, longer-range air-to-air missiles, it will become more difficult for a small expeditionary force to defend friendly airspace effectively and to secure air superiority quickly.

By 2005, a number of regional powers are projected to have fielded fourth-generation fighter-interceptors of the Su-27 Flanker class. The more wealthy among these powers, such as China, may eventually deploy hundreds of these advanced aircraft. Armed with the medium-range AA-12 or similar air-to-air missile, this type of aircraft poses a potent threat to the best U.S. air-to-air fighters. In detailed assessments of air-to-air combat using the Tac Brawler model, Su-27s armed with AA-12s achieved kill potentials of approximately .25 against F-15Cs armed with Advanced Medium Range Air-to-Air Missiles (AMRAAMs). Thus, a flight of six Su-27s might expect to destroy between one and two F-15s in a single sortie—a far higher level of lethality than U.S. fighters have ever encountered. This translates to an exchange ratio of between 3:1 and 6:1 for the F-15Cs against Su-27 Flanker aircraft armed with AA-12s.[2] This rather poor exchange ratio, coupled with the F-15's inability to operate freely over enemy territory covered by radar-guided SAMs, means that up to two weeks might be required to attrit substantially the enemy's force of combat aircraft. And U.S. losses would be high: In the opening days of conflict, U.S. forces might lose as many fighter-interceptors as they deploy to the theater each day. Hence, while the F-15C with AMRAAM retains substantial lethality against

---

[2]In other words, for every F-15C that is lost in air-to-air combat, between three and six Su-27s are downed. See R. D. Shaver, E. R. Harshberger, and N. W. Crawford, *Modernizing Airpower Projection Capabilities: Future Needs and Options*, RAND, IP-126, 1993.

Su-27 Flanker-class aircraft, a small U.S. force of current-generation fighter-interceptors would not be able to prosecute an aggressive campaign against the enemy's air force in the face of these losses. Meanwhile, joint forces would find their deployment ports and airfields under attack while being constrained in their efforts to attack advancing enemy ground forces.

By modernizing its fleet of fighter-interceptors, the U.S. Air Force can ensure that joint forces can quickly gain the freedom to operate even in the face of enemy modernization and stressing, short-warning conflicts. Because of the modernized F-22's ability to engage enemy aircraft before being detected by them, the Su-27's kill potential against the F-22 drops to less than .05, and few friendly aircraft are lost in air-to-air engagements. In fact, the F-22 armed with AMRAAM can achieve exchange ratios upwards of 20:1 against Su-27s. The F-22's high levels of lethality and survivability, coupled with the fact that the F-22 can operate effectively in the vicinity of enemy SAMs, means that a force equipped with aircraft of this nature can achieve a robust air defense posture and air superiority within a few days. Keeping in mind the sensitivity of campaign outcomes to fairly small changes in the time required to enable heavy antiarmor attacks, the value of highly capable air-to-air fighters becomes manifest.

It is worth noting here that judgments about the value of modernizing the U.S. fighter-interceptor fleet, like other modernization programs, should be informed by dynamic assessments of joint capabilities in the context of stressing but plausible future scenarios. A direct comparison of the capabilities of the F-15C versus the Su-27 is of little relevance outside of such a context.

SUPPRESSING SURFACE-TO-AIR DEFENSES

For similar reasons, it is important that DoD continue to enhance capabilities to suppress and destroy the most modern SAM systems. When employed to best effect, modern SAMs such as the SA-10 can provide in-depth protection to key rear area assets, as well as moving coverage of advancing ground forces. The SA-10 and similar systems pose new challenges to defense suppression efforts. Their phased-array radars can be difficult to locate with precision, because they can detect and track aircraft quickly, using adaptive radar waveforms. These high-powered systems are also difficult to jam effectively.

Once located, it takes both a stealthy platform, such as the B-2 or the F-22, and an accurate standoff weapon, such as the Joint Air-to-Surface Standoff Missile (JASSM) or the shorter-range Joint Standoff Weapon (JSOW), to effectively attack the main tracking and guidance radar. This combination is required because of the SA-10's high power, large radar aperture, and attendant long range. Aerial decoys—which can be used to keep the radar on the air for longer periods and, if employed in sufficient numbers, can overwhelm its engagement capacity—are useful additions to this type of attack capability. Standard approaches to SAM suppression, featuring nonstealthy platforms and moderate-range radar homing missiles, while useful against many older SAM systems, are not likely to be effective against competently operated SA-10s and other modern SAMs.

GAINING AND EXPLOITING INFORMATION

It is the nature of power-projection operations that the number of U.S. and allied forces available at the outset of a conflict will be modest in relation to the size of the attacking force. Hence, to be effective in damaging and halting a large-scale armored offensive, expeditionary forces must be highly efficient. A brute force approach to the defense—covering the battlefield with platforms and weapons—is infeasible and, for a host of reasons, undesirable in any case.

Thus, there will be a premium on systems that can locate the main concentrations of enemy maneuver forces, determine the direction and velocity of their movement, and pass this information on to control centers in a timely fashion. The overall objective is to develop operational concepts for targeting moving ground forces that are similar in timeliness and flexibility to current concepts for engaging airborne air forces. Like most air defense sorties, ground attackers would not be launched against specific targets but, rather, would be provided as assets to controllers who, armed with up-to-date information on the location and disposition of enemy ground forces, would assign targets to the attack sorties and provide them with information to assist in the engagement.

Implicit in this approach is the need to distinguish military units, especially armored formations, from clusters of nonmilitary and other unarmored vehicles. To be truly robust in the face of potential countermeasures, such discrimination will probably require multiple types of sensors, such as moving target indicator (MTI) and synthetic aperture (SAR) radars, electro-optical sensors, and passive signals intelligence (SIGINT) collectors. Battlefield surveillance sensors, assessment capabilities, and control centers themselves will need to be rapidly deployable or, in some cases, "virtually" deployable. One way to ensure rapid availability of certain capabilities is to set up staffs in one or two central locations to which theater forces "reach back" for support. Given robust, real-time communication links of sufficient capacity, data from theater-based sensors can be sent to these staffs and processed there, with information then sent back to users in the theater.

In light of these requirements, it is difficult to understand the rationale behind DoD's decision, announced as part of the Quadrennial Defense Review, to reduce from 19 to 13 the number of JSTARS surveillance and battle management aircraft to be fielded. Eight to ten of these aircraft will need to be deployed forward to maintain two continuous orbits in an overseas theater, and there is no immediate substitute system that offers the full range of capabilities provided by this system. Whatever path is chosen, DoD clearly will need to expand its wide-area surveillance capabilities, along with the assessment and control functions needed to make best use of the data provided by these sensors.

RAPIDLY DESTROYING ARMOR

We have seen that the ability of a given force to halt an enemy invasion depends upon modern antiarmor munitions. Sortie effectiveness can be increased by factors of ten or more when newer weapons are substituted for older, unguided weapons. The question then arises: How many of these advanced antiarmor weapons are sufficient to halt two nearly simultaneous invasions?

Figure 5.3 compares the number of antiarmor weapons used by joint forces in three variants of our basic scenario—each of which resulted in a rapid halt of the invasion. The left bar shows the antiarmor weapons used in the halt phase of a scenario featuring the "heroic"

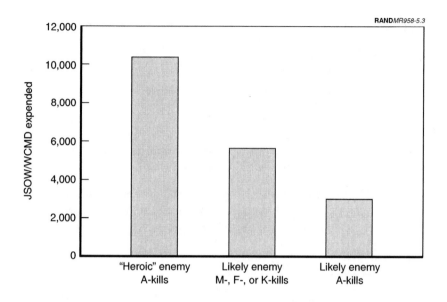

Figure 5.3—Larger Quantities of Area Antiarmor Munitions Are Needed

adversary, where each unit presses the attack at a high rate of speed until more than 70 percent of its armored vehicles have been damaged or destroyed. In this case, U.S. forces required nearly 10,500 WCMD and JSOW weapons dispensing smart, antiarmor bomblets (along with a number of ATACMS missiles and helicopter-delivered Hellfire munitions) to halt the attacker by Day 10.

The other two bars in Figure 5.3 show area antiarmor weapons ex-pended in cases involving our less-heroic opponent, whose forces advance more slowly and are rendered ineffective when 50 percent of their vehicles are damaged or destroyed. If one is satisfied that dam-aging 50 percent of the armored vehicles to an "A-kill" level or better is sufficient, around 3200 area antiarmor munitions would be called for. Alternatively, if one strove for a more-demanding damage criterion of 50 percent M-, F-, or K-kills, some 5700 such weapons would be needed.

Using the middle case as a benchmark, we conclude that DoD should plan to procure a mix of antiarmor weapons, including not fewer than approximately 15,000 smart, air-delivered area antiarmor weapons to be able to defeat armored offensives in two major theater wars and still have reserve stocks for subsequent phases of these or other operations. This inventory goal is more than twice what the Air Force, Navy and Marine Corps are currently planning to procure by 2005.[3] Remarkably, in DoD assessments of U.S. force structure set in this time frame, many Navy, and Marine Corps sorties allocated to the attack of armored formations are shown to be delivering the Mk-20 Rockeye—a 1960s era unguided cluster weapon of low effectiveness. These must be regarded as, essentially, wasted sorties.

It will be important for the United States to preposition the bulk of these stocks of advanced munitions overseas so that scarce inter-theater airlift assets, which are scarce, are not needed to move the munitions in the opening days of the conflict.[4]

---

[3]These weapons figures assume a weapon similar in capability to the WCMD-delivered or JSOW-delivered sensor fuzed weapon examined here. There are many options for area antiarmor munitions, including the Brilliant Antitank Weapon (BAT) and the developmental Low-Cost Anti Armor Submunition (LOCAAS). By all accounts, these weapons will be at least as effective as SFW and may be less costly. Whatever the individual weapons chosen, it is clear that U.S. capabilities *and budgets* must be increased in this area.

[4]In our baseline scenario, 1400 WCMD/Skeet weapons are needed to attack 140 kilometers of armored column every day. To deliver just these weapons from the United States to a theater as distant as the Persian Gulf would require approximately 30 C-141B equivalent sorties per day, or around one-third of the total daily airlift effort.

Chapter Six

BROADER IMPLICATIONS FOR THE DEFENSE PROGRAM

Given the military capabilities fielded by current adversaries, U.S. forces today seem well prepared to deter and defeat large-scale aggression against important U.S. interests. But our adversaries— current and potential—are not standing still. As their forces begin to field new, more-capable weapons, U.S. forces could witness an erosion in their ability to "defeat large-scale, cross-border aggression in two distant theaters in overlapping time frames," as called for in the administration's defense strategy. The reason is not, as some have asserted, that U.S. force structure in the aggregate will be too small to do the job. Rather, the shortfalls revealed by our analysis are mainly qualitative rather than quantitative.

Since the early 1990s, funding for defense modernization has been hard pressed. DoD's procurement budget in Fiscal Year (FY) 1996 was one-third lower, in real terms, than in FY80.[1] As we have seen, growing resource constraints have meant that programs central to the effectiveness of early arriving forces are either underfunded (e.g., Skeet antiarmor munitions) or being truncated (JSTARS). Indications are that pressure on these accounts is likely to grow.

DoD's approach to addressing this problem, chiefly by seeking to reduce unneeded base structure and to accelerate the adoption of new and more-efficient approaches to many of its support activities, is laudable. Eventually, such measures can yield substantial savings

---

[1]David S.C. Chu, "What Can Likely Defense Budgets Sustain?" in Zalmay M. Khalilzad and David A. Ochmanek (eds.), *Strategic Appraisal 1997: Strategy and Defense Planning for the 21st Century*, RAND, MR-826-AF, 1997, p. 260.

that could be applied to higher-priority activities. But most of these initiatives will take time to implement, and even more time will be needed before many of them begin to pay large dividends. Thus, even if DoD is highly successful in reducing its costs of doing business, savings will need to be generated from other accounts over the next five to ten years to field all of the capabilities needed to halt invasions in two theaters nearly simultaneously.

PAYING FOR NEEDED ENHANCEMENTS

It is highly likely that further, deeper reductions in endstrength (personnel) and force structure will be unavoidable a few years hence if DoD attempts to meet its highest priority modernization needs. How should those cuts be apportioned to avoid or minimize a loss of warfighting capability?

DoD has recognized that the most obvious place to cut military manpower and force structure is in units that play little or no role in current or projected theater operations—that is, nondeployable forces. The primary examples of these forces today are the air defense squadrons of the Air National Guard and the Army National Guard's combat-configured brigades and divisions. DoD has proposed reductions in both forces. The Air Force will convert six continental air defense squadrons to general-purpose missions and will eliminate some three larger squadrons from its active force structure. The Secretary of Defense announced a reduction of 15,000 military personnel from the Army's active component and 45,000 military personnel from the Army's reserve component. Previous to the QDR, 12 of the Army National Guard's 40 brigades already were scheduled to change from combat to combat support capability. Once in place, these manpower cuts could save approximately $450 million annually. Such cuts are welcome, and they yield no real reduction in U.S. military capabilities.

However, these cuts cannot, by themselves, yield sufficient savings to ensure a robust force modernization program. Given the marginal utility of combat-configured units in the Army's reserve component, substantially greater reductions seem justified. Nevertheless, political opposition to such changes may delay or limit the realization of savings. And even if the savings are eventually realized from cuts to nondeploying forces and support activities, the price tag associated with recapitalizing the entire force structure called for in the QDR might still exceed available funds. In either case, DoD could well find itself a few years hence again facing the need to cut the active and readily deployable reserve component force structure. The approach taken in this report and its supporting analysis provide some clear directions that can help inform such cuts.

As DoD has recognized, it is essential that capabilities needed to quickly execute the halt phase of future conflicts be retained and, as necessary, enhanced. U.S. adversaries are likely to realize that the opening phase of a future conflict will determine the cost, nature, and duration of the conflict. Thus, a U.S. force that is postured and equipped to deny the enemy the prospect of success in a short-notice attack is most likely to be the best deterrent against such an attempt.

In its 1993 Bottom-Up Review, DoD identified a "building block" of forces from each of the services that it used for planning purposes to describe the type and number of forces that would be required to defeat aggression against a major regional opponent. That building block, reproduced in Figure 6.1, generally describes the type of force that DoD today would plan to send to a major theater war.[2] DoD's total warfighting force structure, which is approximately twice this building block, is assumed to be capable of fighting and winning two nearly simultaneous MTWs. When most planners consider cuts in force structure, they think in terms of across-the-board, vertical cuts to this service-denominated building block. Guidance to the services regarding their fiscal planning and authorized force structure is also issued in these terms.

In light of DoD's emphasis on the need to prevail in the opening phase of a future conflict, however, a more useful way to conceptualize MTW building blocks is shown in Figure 6.2. This approach is based not on systems or units provided by each military service, but rather on the functions provided by those force elements in defending against large-scale combined arms attacks—the most demanding and important missions assigned to U.S. forces. Taking this approach, it is possible to identify three types of deployable forces:

---

[2]See Aspin, 1993, pp. 18–19.

RAND*MR958-6.1*

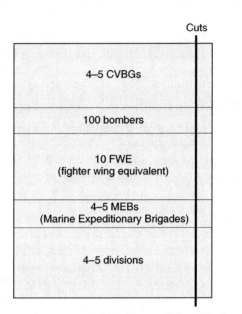

Figure 6.1—The MTW Building Block

RAND*MR958-6.2*

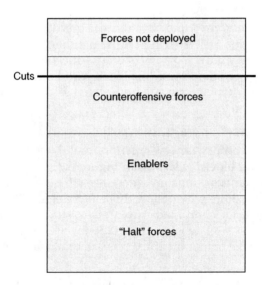

Figure 6.2—A Functional MTW Building Block

- Those that contribute to the initial phase (as well as succeeding phases) of the operation;

- Those that provide key enabling functions throughout the operation; and

- Those that are available only for the later counterattack or counteroffensive phase, in which enemy forces would be forcibly expelled from captured territory.

From the perspective of preparing for major theater warfare, it seems clear that if cuts must be taken from force structure, they should be taken horizontally from those forces that are not a part of the deployed force or from those that arrive late and contribute only to the counteroffensive.

We advocate this approach not only because of the manifest importance of halting early, though that should be reason enough. This approach is warranted also because incipient and forthcoming improvements in the capabilities of modern information and firepower systems suggest changes in the division of labor among different types of forces. As we have seen, these improvements are allowing modest-sized forward deployed and early arriving forces—the halt forces and the enablers—to engage and quickly destroy, at least under some conditions, a far greater portion of the enemy's warfighting capabilities than has heretofore been possible. Consequently, the role of forces committed to the later phases of a major theater war is changing.

This judgment is based on growing evidence that longer-range firepower can be substantially more effective than in the past, not only in the halt phase of a theater war but also after the enemy ground force has halted and dug in. Modern navigation and engagement systems can permit fixed- and rotary-wing aircraft to find and attack targets effectively at night. Coupled with accurate weapons, this means that U.S. forces can harass stationary forces and interdict enemy troop and supply movements virtually around the clock and in poor weather as well as fair. As the air campaign in Operation Desert

Storm showed, unremitting attacks of this nature can sap an enemy force of the capability and will to fight.[3]

In the future, then, planners will see later-arriving forces (principally composed of mobile ground force units) as increasingly providing the joint commander with the means to ensure that the enemy ground forces, badly mauled by joint firepower, move from their dug-in positions, either to fight or flee. Once dislodged, the enemy forces become more susceptible to detection and engagement by a wide range of U.S. sensors and fires. In short, where the traditional concept of maneuver warfare saw the close battle as the decisive element of the joint campaign, future commanders will see the halting operation—by necessity and choice dominated by standoff sensors and longer-range fires—as the culminating point of the conflict. Put another way, traditional doctrine saw *fire as enabling maneuver*: Fire was the means, shaping the battlefield to support the end of maneuver so that friendly forces could enjoy advantages of surprise or favorable position in the close battle. In the future, the dominant paradigm will be *information enabling effective firepower*. Gaining accurate, timely, and comprehensive information about the location and disposition of enemy forces, and denying comparable information to the enemy, will become perhaps the single most important element of a successful campaign.

Even in the conflict's opening phase, friendly ground forces will play key roles: By their presence in the theater, friendly armor can compel the enemy to attack with sizable formations of heavy mechanized forces. This attack is actually advantageous to the defenders, because it makes it more likely that U.S. surveillance assets will detect prewar mobilization efforts and that, once on the move, the enemy ground forces will be slower and more cumbersome than light unarmored forces would be. Friendly heavy forces are uniquely able to "stand and fight" in defense of critical territory. Using delay and retrograde tactics, mobile friendly ground forces can slow an advancing enemy and create more lucrative targets for longer-range fires. Nevertheless, as U.S. information and firepower continue to improve, we envisage a substantial shift in the division of labor away

---

[3]For an assessment of the effects of U.S. air operations on enemy morale and willingness to fight, see Steven T. Hosmer, *Psychological Effects of U.S. Air Operations in Four Wars, 1941–1991: Lessons for U.S. Commanders,* RAND, MR-576-AF, 1996.

from heavy ground forces and toward longer-range firepower in many situations.

Figure 6.3 presents a somewhat more detailed description of the types of forces and assets that might typically constitute halt, enabler, and counteroffensive forces in a major theater operation.

Many of the systems most needed to provide two robust halt and enable forces are already substantially funded, especially the major platforms, such as the C-17 airlifter and the F-22 fighter. The capabilities most at risk to budget-driven delays generally reside in less-conspicuous programs that do not define major force elements. These include

- Advanced munitions, such as smart antiarmor munitions and standoff attack weapons,

- Sensor-to-controller-to-shooter communication links,

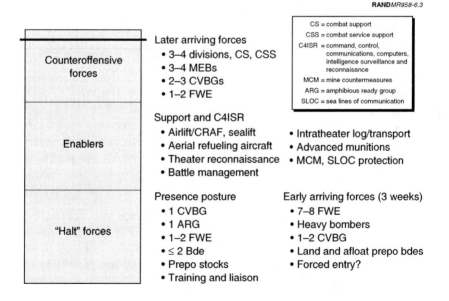

Figure 6.3—Forces and Functions for a Major Theater War

- Upgrades to avionics and other systems on existing platforms that will allow them to integrate and employ advanced information and munitions,

- Theater surveillance sensors and platforms, to locate and characterize both enemy maneuver forces and mobile air defenses,

- Prepositioned assets, and

- Improved concepts and capabilities for finding, engaging, and destroying advanced surface-to-air missile systems, such as the SA-10.

In our rough estimation, additional sustained investments of $2 billion–2.5 billion per year in these capabilities over a ten-year period should suffice to avoid further debilitating delays and cancellations in these low-profile but critical areas. Fairly modest cuts in later-arriving forces—on the order of 10 to 15 percent—should suffice to generate these funds.

Clearly, halting an invasion is not the same as victory, even if the halt comes quickly. U.S. and allied forces in future wars will be charged with other important objectives as well, including reducing the war-making capacity of the enemy nation, expelling enemy forces from captured territory, compelling surrender, and, perhaps, occupying enemy territory in order to impose a postwar settlement. In some cases, these objectives will call for forces well beyond those required for successful early operations. But halting the invasion (and, by extension, gaining dominance over operations on the land and sea, and in the air and space) creates favorable conditions for the pursuit of other objectives.

In short, modest cuts in later-arriving forces, with the resulting savings focused on early arrivers, would yield a force more capable of defeating short-warning invasions, yet retaining the capacity to expel enemy ground forces from captured territory. There need be no reduction in the number or the capabilities of U.S. ground forces available for a single major theater war. Two to three divisions plus a Marine Expeditionary Force would remain in the active component for operations in a second MTW as well.

Of course, U.S. forces must be capable of conducting a wider range of operations over a wider range of circumstances than those considered in this analysis. These operations may include peacekeeping, intervention, monitoring, and sanction enforcement operations of extended duration. DoD will need to consider the potential future demand for these and other operations when weighing priorities for overall force structure and modernization needs. We believe that providing forces for large-scale power projection is the proper centerpiece for U.S. force planning in the coming era and that the scenario and cases examined here represent a prudent basis for evaluating those forces.

CONCLUDING OBSERVATIONS

By developing new operational concepts that exploit advanced capabilities—for gathering and passing information; for large numbers of smart, specialized munitions; for stealth; and for other innovations—U.S. military forces are on the threshold of realizing a revolution in the conduct of large-scale theater warfare. These innovations promise to allow U.S. forces to prevail in power projection operations against future adversaries even under stressing conditions. Alternatively, should we fail to exploit these emerging capabilities and hew to a more traditional approach, future U.S. commanders could find themselves unable to contend with well-equipped and competent regional adversaries at costs and risks that are acceptable to U.S. leaders.

Projecting large-scale military power into an aggressor's back yard is never easy. By focusing on the dynamics of the opening phase of future conflicts, we can learn more about the demands of that critical phase and about nascent opportunities to ensure that U.S. forces can prevail. For sound political and economic reasons, the United States no longer stations large formations of forces abroad on a routine basis as we did in Central Europe during the Cold War. And our adversaries cannot be relied upon to be so foolish as to give U.S. military forces weeks to build up in the theater. Moreover, as weapons of mass destruction and the means to deliver them proliferate, the risks of placing large numbers of U.S. military personnel within range of these weapons will escalate inexorably. *For these reasons, a traditional approach to theater warfare that relies primarily on heavy maneuver forces to halt and destroy the bulk of the enemy's attacking ground force in the close battle can no longer be regarded as an appropriate means of supporting U.S. objectives in the opening weeks of future conflicts.*

New, emerging concepts will allow modestly sized forward forces and rapidly deploying units to play a far greater role in locating, disrupting, destroying, and halting attacking maneuver forces—and, more broadly, in gaining dominance over enemy operations. By exploiting information and advanced munitions, these concepts will allow the bulk of the enemy's combat power to be neutralized at extended ranges, rather than in direct fire engagements with, or in close proximity to, friendly ground forces. These concepts are well suited to meeting the demands of U.S. strategy for power projection. If fully supported, these concepts can support a defense posture that strengthens deterrence and, should deterrence fail, provides the means for U.S. forces to gain the initiative rapidly and to prevail in conflict.

Changes of this magnitude in the capabilities of longer-range surveillance and firepower systems represent a fundamentally new approach to theater warfare. As these new capabilities are developed, tested, and fielded, they should prompt a thorough review of our operational concepts, force mix, and investment priorities.

ASSESSMENT APPROACH AND METHODS

Many theater warfare simulations (e.g. TACWAR, TAC THUNDER, JICM, etc.) assess the ability of armored forces to move forward in the face of armed opposition from air, land, and naval forces. These methods can simulate not only the halt phase of campaigns but also the subsequent "build and pound" and counterattack phases of theater wars. These models also seek to encompass many other major components of a joint campaign.

For a close examination of firepower effects against enemy ground forces in the halt phase, many of these calculations are superfluous. This is especially true in situations where ground forces available for the defense are few in number and widely dispersed. In light of these drawbacks to the standard assessment tools, we set out to develop some simple, transparent tools that would better reflect the conditions prevalent in the opening phase of future conflicts and that could allow analysts as well as consumers of these analyses to grasp readily the relationships between input assumptions and outputs. These factors have been coded into a set of simple calculation spreadsheets.

Such tools provide a straightforward method for exploring the capability of firepower systems under various conditions. While not definitive—the uncertainty in some inputs is significant—we believe that these calculations are capable of reflecting the dynamics among many of the most significant factors bearing on outcomes in the halt phase of the scenarios we examined and, hence, offer insights on the capabilities and limitations of joint forces in the most critical portion of a conflict.

CONCEPTUAL MODEL

The Attacking Force

The advancing mechanized force is depicted as arrays of armored vehicles moving forward along multiple axes of advance. In reality, the forces on each axis will be moving down road networks (or, in some cases, off of roads) in unit formations. At the tactical level, such a situation is similar to that shown in Figure A.1.

The enemy's mechanized units will consist of intermixed armored vehicles and "thin-skinned" vehicles (trucks, etc.), with the armored vehicles seeking to maintain a minimum spacing in accordance with doctrine. For a large force, the forward rate of the entire force is largely a function of the capacity of the available lines of communication and the need to maintain a semblance of march integrity, the combination of which inflicts "friction" on the movement of large ground forces. In most cases, the combination of these factors will

RAND*MR958-A.1*

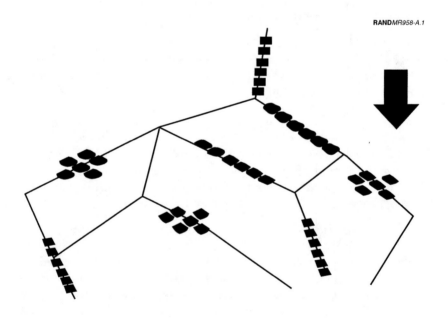

Figure A.1—Tactical View of the Advancing Armored Force

mean that the overall force moves at a rate significantly slower than the maximum movement rate of the individual vehicles on the road at any one time.

This situation, which is rather complicated at the tactical level, can be modeled in a simplified way at the operational level. First, a series of assumptions are made:

- Advancing units move forward at a constant rate determined by the capacity of the available lines of communication

- Units are observed and localized by wide-area surveillance and reconnaissance assets, and

- Units are within range of attack by forces using area antiarmor munitions.

In such a circumstance, each advancing unit can be treated as a simple length of column to be attacked, rather than as distinct vehicles. Moreover, the precise location of each unit is irrelevant (all are within range of attack); instead, the important issue becomes the total number of units (or, more precisely, total *length* of units) to be attacked. Each main axis of advance can be envisioned as a "conveyor belt" or chain of vehicles of a given length, as shown in Figure A.2. The length of the chain is determined by the number of armored vehicles and their spacing.

Damage Criteria and "Halting"

Advancing units are assumed to stop moving forward when they incur a stated level of damage. All other units move forward without regard to the overall level of attrition until they are attacked. From the defender's point of view, this is an extremely conservative assumption, as the attack of some units is likely to choke and litter roads, damage fuel and repair assets, confuse and damage command and control functions, and weaken morale.

Because each unit is treated as a length of column to be attacked, attacks against each main axis are accomplished by achieving a given damage expectancy against each kilometer of the total advancing force. Several factors can affect the rate at which U.S. forces can attack, some of which are shown in Figure A.3.

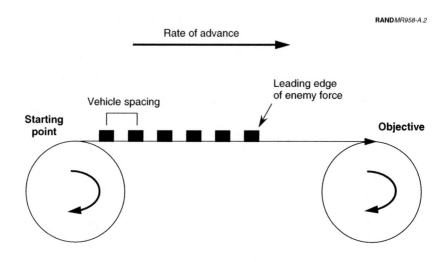

Figure A.2—A Simplified, Operational-Level View of Each Axis of an Advancing Armored Force

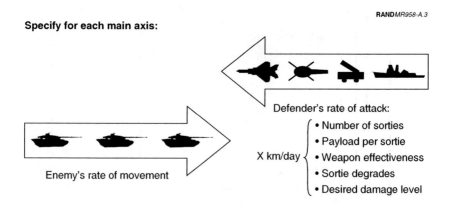

Figure A.3—Factors Affecting Rate of Attack

In this approach, the key measure of the enemy's advance is the net distance that unattacked forces have moved each day. For each day, the calculation of this net advance is one of competing rates—enemy rate of advance, measured in kilometers per day, competing with the rate of attack to a specified (high) level of damage, also measured in kilometers per day. Because the enemy advance is assumed to be "frictionless," the calculation is a simple subtraction of attack rate from advance rate. At some high rates of attack, this quantity can be negative; that is, the U.S. forces "attack down the road" at a rate faster than enemy forces move forward.

Relation to Other Constructs

Note that this conceptual picture of the armored force (a movement-constrained force, capable of pushing a limited amount of its total capability forward each day) is quite different from many other constructs. Many models of armored advance consider large amounts of armored force (divisions, corps) as a single aggregated "block," that moves forward at some rate until a given fraction of total force is destroyed. For example, using the block construct, the force of 9600 vehicles in the base case of our analysis would move forward at a constant rate until $.7 \times 9600 = 6912$ vehicles were destroyed.

Baseline movement rates attributed to these large aggregations of force are often similar to those we assume, but these baseline rates are rarely applied. Forces opposed by fires or maneuver are assumed to slow down, often to movement rates much slower than those we posit. Even so, the block approach tends to exaggerate the difficulty in halting a force with firepower. This is because, under the block assumption, damage to the opponent (from firepower or other sources) does not slow the force until quite large amounts of force are applied. For instance, in our baseline case, we do not reach the stated 70 percent damage threshold for the entire force until Day 10. Assuming a 40-kilometer-per-day advance (slower than our baseline case), the block construct would advance 400 kilometers. In our construction, where firepower impedes advance, the "high-water mark" of advance, 260 kilometers, is reached on Day 6. All of this would be of mere academic interest, except for the fact that the simple block construct underlies many large theater models, including TACWAR.[1]

---

[1]There is some compensation for this difference, however. The "break point" for large force aggregations is often set lower than 70 percent, typically around 50 percent, sometimes less. Presumably, the basis for assuming a break point for large forces has less to do with individual unit cohesion and initiative. Instead, one might posit

The differences between the two approaches vary with level of aggregation and other assumptions. For highly aggregated forces (divisions or corps), the approach used here can be made equivalent to the block approach if one assumes that there are many axes of advance (in most cases, one must assume 15–20 axes to get rough equivalency). This has the effect of moving more and more force to the front edge of the attack. Likewise, the block approach approximates the approach we advocate if the armored forces are treated at lower levels of aggregation (brigade or company).

Clearly, there is no universally "right" answer—the validity of these approaches will vary with circumstance. However, we believe that the approach we use in this analysis adequately captures the dynamics of the cases we believe most important: a rapid advance of armored forces, reasonably constrained by geography, and opposed primarily by effective firepower.

CALCULATING ANTIARMOR EFFECTIVENESS FOR LIMITED-AREA WEAPONS

The following describes our assumptions and calculations regarding the effectiveness of the BLU-108 Skeet antiarmor submunition delivered by fixed-wing aircraft against columns of armored vehicles on the move.

Effects of One Dispenser Against an Armored Column

In numerous operational and lot acceptance tests at Eglin Air Force Base and elsewhere, single sensor fuzed weapons (SFW), each with 40 Skeet bomblets, have been dropped from aircraft onto columns of vehicles. These columns consist of a mix of armored vehicles— tanks, infantry fighting vehicles (IFVs), and self-propelled artillery— and trucks bearing heat sources that simulate hot engines for the infrared seekers on the Skeet bomblets. The armored vehicles are spaced approximately 50 meters apart, with the trucks interspersed

---

overwhelming logistic difficulties or a failure of initiative on the part of higher-level commanders. See Paul K. Davis and Manuel Carrillo, *Exploratory Analysis of "the Halt Problem": A Briefing on Methods and Initial Insights*, RAND, DB-232-OSD, 1997.

among them. As shown in Figure A.4, when delivered at high speed and low altitude, the 40 Skeets arrive at their targets in an elliptical pattern that is approximately 400 meters long and 200 meters wide.

Table A.1 shows the results of 27 tests of the SFW conducted between 1993 (when SFW completed its initial operational test and evaluation [IOT&E]) and 1997.[2] It shows that, on average, a single SFW scores more than five hits on between three and four armored vehicles. Given normal delivery errors and the fact that not all vehicles hit will be seriously damaged, we judge that approximately one half of the armored vehicles within the SFW pattern will be damaged to at least an "availability-kill" (A-kill) criterion (at least one critical component

RAND*MR958-A.4*

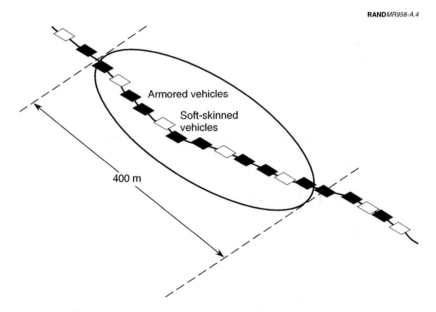

Figure A.4—Footprint of Sensor Fuzed Weapon in Operational Tests: 50-Meter Spacing Between Armored Vehicles

---

[2]These are all of the tests of the SFW in this period in which the dispenser was released from a level delivery and for which confirmed data on the number of vehicles hit could be gathered.

Table A.1

Tests of Sensor Fuzed Weapon, 1993–1997

Date	Targets Hit[a]		Total Hits[a]
	Armored	Trucks	
5/11/93	7/4	—	7/4
6/23/93	8/4	1/1	9/5
6/29/93	5/3	3/1	8/4
7/7/93	5/4	1/1	6/5
4/26/94	4/3	—	4/3
5/18/94	4/3	1/1	5/4
5/24/94	8/5	2/1	1/6
6/28/94	3/2	1/1	4/3
8/18/94	8/3	2/1	10/4
9/26/94	6/4	2/2	8/6
10/14/94	3/3	2/1	5/4
11/15/94	4/2	1/1	5/3
1/10/95	5/3	—	5/3
2/1/95	5/5	—	5/5
5/23/95	6/4	2/1	8/5
6/20/95	7/3	1/1	8/4
7/12/95	3/3	2/1	5/4
10/17/95	4/2	1/1	5/3
12/18/95	1/1	3/2	4/3
1/25/96	2/1	—	2/1
3/8/96	4/3	1/1	5/4
8/5/96	4/4	1/1	5/5
11/16/96	7/4	3/1	10/5
1/22/97	7/5	—	7/5
3/11/97	7/5	1/1	8/6
4/29/97	3/2	1/1	4/3
5/28/97	9/3	4/1	13/4
Total	139/88	36/23	175/111
Average	5.1/3.3	1.3/.8	6.5/4.1

[a]The two numbers given for each entry under "Targets Hit" and "Total Hits" refer first to the number of hits on vehicles and then to the number of vehicles that were hit. In the test on May 11, 1993, for example, the entry "7/4" denotes that there were 7 hits on 4 armored vehicles; there were no hits on trucks.

would need repair, compelling the tank to be removed from the line of march and repaired).[3]

---

[3]See Chapter Four for a discussion of the A-kill criterion.

We also assume in our calculations an enemy that is even more disciplined and dispersed, with average spacing of 100 meters between armored vehicles. In this case, an optimally delivered SFW would be expected to cover four armored vehicles within its footprint, yielding $4 \times 0.5 = 2$ armored vehicles damaged per accurately delivered dispenser.

In most of the operational and lot acceptance tests, aircraft delivered tactical munitions dispensers (TMDs) from a level plane of attack and aligned them with the column of vehicles. To account for turns in the road, suboptimal alignment, offsets, and other practical considerations of weapon delivery under conditions of combat, we reduced the effective footprint of the average delivered weapon in our assessments by one-third. As depicted in Figure A.5, the effective pattern length in these assessments is assumed to be $400 \times 0.67 \approx 270$ meters. At 100-meter spacing, therefore, 2.7 armored vehicles would be expected to appear in the footprint, and a single weapon would

RAND*MR958-A.5*

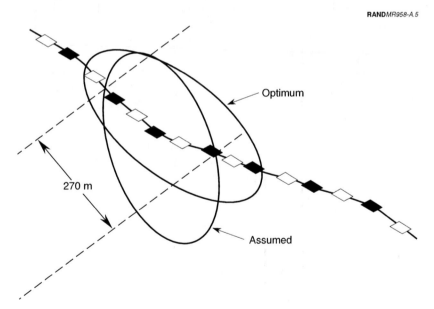

Figure A.5—Pattern Degraded by Delivery Error: 100-Meter Spacing Between Armored Vehicles

damage $2.7 \times 0.5 = 1.35$ of these vehicles. This, then, is the kill potential per weapon for a spacing of 100 meters and a degrade of one-third for delivery errors.

Effects of Multiple Dispensers on an Armored Column

The next step involves scaling up from one dispenser on a column to multiple dispensers. As noted in Chapter Four, our baseline assumption for pulling armored units (of a "heroic" enemy) out of the line of march is when the attacker damages at least 70 percent of the armored vehicles in that unit. In our calculations, we contend that we have "serviced" one kilometer of column when the damage expectancy (DE) within that kilometer exceeds 70 percent.

In scaling up, weapons delivery can be assessed according to whether the dispensers are deployed in an ordered manner or in an unordered manner. Ordered fire in this case refers to the delivery of weapons such that their footprints precisely overlap to provide double coverage, but no more, along the kilometer of road. The calculus for damage expectancy with ordered fire is $1 - (1 - P_k)^w$, where P_k is probability of kill and w is the number of weapons per aimpoint. To achieve DE > 0.7, w must equal approximately 2; that is, $1 - (1 - 0.5)^2 = 0.75$. Thus, about seven weapons are required to achieve this damage expectancy over a kilometer of road ($1000 \div 270 \times 2 \approx 7$); see the top portion of Figure A.6.

At the opposite end of the spectrum, unordered fire accounts for the "fog of war," whereby factors such as target engagement problems and weapon inaccuracies further degrade the effectiveness of the weapons. Weapons are distributed randomly, and some segments of column are triple-covered while other segments are uncovered. To calculate the effectiveness of unordered fire, we use the exponential approximation:

$$DE = 1 - e^{-n\lambda},$$

where n is the number of weapons per kilometer and λ is the weapon's effective pattern length (0.27 kilometers) multiplied by the portion of armored vehicles damaged under a pattern (approximately 50 percent). In this case, using random, or unordered

RAND*MR958-A.6*

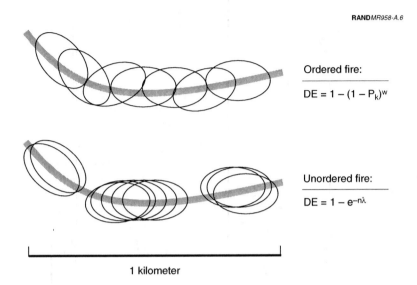

Ordered fire:

$$DE = 1 - (1 - P_k)^w$$

Unordered fire:

$$DE = 1 - e^{-n\lambda}$$

1 kilometer

Figure A.6—Reduced Effectiveness of TMDs Using Random Delivery

fire, we reach the desired damage expectancy at ten weapons per kilometer; that is:

$$1 - e^{-(10)(0.5)(0.27)} = 0.74$$

Unordered fire is depicted in the bottom portion of Figure A.6.

We believe that actual capability, particularly by the middle of the next decade, should permit delivery that is far more effective than unordered fire and may even approach ordered fire. Indeed, within a few years, the Air Force's inventory of SFWs, which deliver Skeet bomblets in an unguided tactical munitions dispenser, will be replaced by wind-corrected munitions dispensers (WCMDs), which can be guided to their aimpoints by an inertial navigation device. Nevertheless, to avoid the risk of overstating the effectiveness of this new weapon, we assume in our calculations that aircraft delivering WCMD and Skeet achieve results no better than those of unordered fire. Thus, we apply ten weapons per kilometer to "service" each kilometer-long segment of armored column. Note that this calculation is independent of vehicle spacing: Within limits, approximately 70 percent of the armored vehicles on that kilometer of road are damaged to an A-kill standard, irrespective of the density of vehicles on the road.

To test the accuracy of the exponential approximation as applied to multiple WCMD deliveries, we enlisted the aid of analysts from Textron Defense Systems, producer of the SFW. Textron applied its simulation model of Skeet submunitions in attacks on columns of vehicles and plotted the results in terms of DE and numbers of weapons per kilometer, given three levels of delivery accuracy, expressed in terms of circular error probable (CEP). Textron compared these results with the exponential approximation using the assumptions stated above. The outcome is plotted in Figure A.7.

Figure A.7 displays Textron simulations using 0-meter, 30-meter, and 60-meter CEPs. The exponential approximation ("e-function") appears as the darker curve second from the bottom. Under our assumptions, the approximation equates to a CEP of about 55 meters.

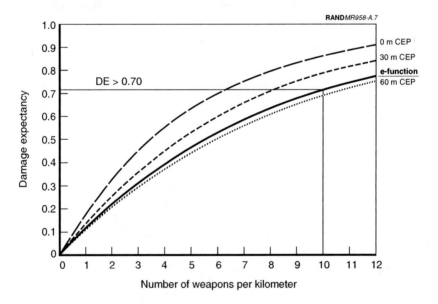

Figure A.7—Comparing Our Exponential Approximation
with Textron's Simulations

The WCMD is expected to achieve an accuracy of 30 meters CEP or better. Thus, the exponential approximation, in combination with our assumptions about pattern size, the projection of each pattern on the road, and portion of armored vehicles damaged under the pattern, yields results somewhat below those achieved in Textron's simulations: Where we apply ten dispensers (with 400 smart submunitions) per kilometer to achieve a DE in excess of 0.7, by Textron's estimates (using a 30-meter CEP), the WCMD should be able to achieve the same DE with only eight weapons per kilometer.

Applying Sorties to Slow the Rate of Armored Advance

The final part of the calculus is to apply attack sorties against kilometers of armored columns to achieve a DE of 0.7 or better on each unit attacked. The greater the number of kilometers of column that firepower can service, the slower the rate of advance of unattacked enemy armor. When firepower's daily capacity to attack armored columns (at DE > 0.7) on a given axis equals the unimpeded rate of armored advance (in our case, 70 kilometers per day), the actual rate of advance of unattacked vehicles on that axis drops to zero. In our vernacular, *the armored advance along this axis is halted*—i.e., the armored advance has reached its "high-water mark."

We invoke an operational degrade against sorties (as opposed to weapons effectiveness) to account for factors that might prevent an aircraft from attacking a valid target—e.g., failure to link up with aerial tankers when necessary, failure to be assigned a valid target, attacks on columns of non-armored vehicles, etc. We degrade sorties by more than one-third; so only 57 percent of all sorties tasked to attack armor actually do so—at which time the exponential approximation is applied in relation to weapons effectiveness.

Let us now apply sorties to a column moving 70 kilometers per day. Figure A.8 shows that an armored force would take five days to travel 350 kilometers if unimpeded. If we send 82 F-15E sorties per day against this advance, $82 \times 0.57 \approx 47$ F-15E sorties will deliver weapons on their intended targets. At eight SFWs per sortie, 376 weapons per day are applied against the columns. Thus, the 82 F-15E sorties can service $376 \div 10 = 38$ kilometers of column per day. The net rate of armored advance therefore diminishes to $70 - 38 = 32$ kilometers per

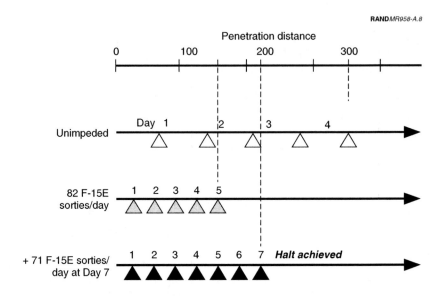

Figure A.8—Calculating Penetration Distance

day. The advance would reach only 160 kilometers in five days given 82 F-15E sorties per day (or 47 effective sorties per day).

In general, as more sorties arrive in the theater, the enemy is further delayed, and when the capacity to attack armored columns exceeds 70 kilometers per day along a main axis of advance (in the baseline case), the enemy is deemed "halted" (he reaches his "high-water mark").[4] In this example, a halt would be achieved when approximately 153 F-15E sorties per day are available for attacks on that axis ($153 \times 0.57 \approx 87$ effective sorties carrying eight TMDs each, or 696 total, giving about 70 kilometers of road serviced per day with ten TMDs per kilometer). A halt is achieved on Day 7, as depicted on the bottom line of Figure A.8, when 71 additional F-15E sorties are applied per day on that particular axis.

---

[4]In cases that fail to generate 70 kilometers' worth of daily attack sorties along each main axis of advance, the halt is assumed to occur when all of the enemy's armored columns have been damaged to a level of 70 percent.

In addition, we recognize that the enemy will attempt to repair damaged armored vehicles and return them to the line of march. These efforts increase the number of sorties required to halt an enemy force. In our calculations, we assume that the enemy can immediately repair some damaged vehicles at a constant rate.[5] This assumption probably overstates the ability of the enemy to repair damaged vehicles. Maintenance units, which accompany or closely follow maintenance units, will be subjected to the same air attacks as the armored vehicles they are assigned to repair. This will impede the rate at which these maintenance units can conduct repairs, as well as reduce their repair capacity through attrition of repair vehicles, crews, and stocks. Continued, massive air attacks will, in all likelihood, swamp remaining repair capacity. Moreover, repaired vehicles reinserted into the line of march will be expected to increase the density of columns and, hence, increase their vulnerability.

Figure A.9 provides a template for determining both the penetration distance of an invading force with a constant repair rate depending on the rate of weapon employment by the defending force. It is as an easy, "on-the-fly" way to calculate effects of antiarmor attacks.

While maintaining the baseline assumptions of DE > 0.7, 100-meter spacing, and 9600 total armored vehicles, we increase the number of axes of advance to five and reduce the unimpeded rate of advance to 50 kilometers per day. The x-axis shows the number of days, and the y-axis depicts the cumulative number of SFW employed. The latter variable readily can be translated into sorties of various types of strike aircraft.

The template demonstrates that for an enemy force advancing along five axes with an unimpeded movement rate of 50 kilometers per day and a requirement of 10 weapons per kilometer to achieve a damage

---

[5]This is a fairly gross way to represent enemy repair capacity, but it does have the expected effect of prolonging the duration of the halt. Another way of accounting for repair capabilities is to apply the exponential function such that $R_d = D(1 - e^{-RP/D})$, where R_d is the number of vehicles repaired per day, D is the number of vehicles damaged per day, and RP is the repair potential. If RP = 100 and D = 250, R_1 = 82 (82 vehicles are repaired at the end of Day 1). On Day 2, another 250 vehicles are damaged, which, when added to the 168 vehicles from Day 1 that were not repaired, yields R_2 = 89. Future efforts will, in all likelihood, apply this approach.

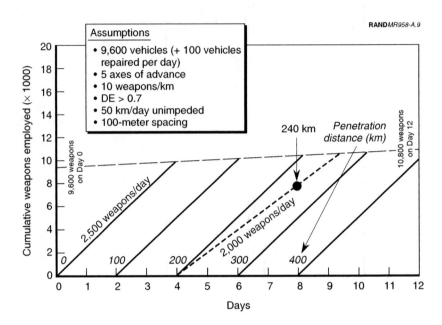

Figure A.9—A Template for Determining Penetration Distance and Weapons per Day

expectancy greater than 0.7, 2500 weapons per day are required to stay on a par with the advancing armor. This rate of weapons employment is depicted by the set of slanted, solid lines. If we begin heavy antiarmor attacks on Day 4 at this rate, we can hold the enemy at a penetration distance of 200 kilometers. Alternatively, if we can apply only 2000 weapons per day beginning on Day 4, we can slow the enemy's rate of advance to ten kilometers per day. Thus, at the end of eight days, the enemy will have penetrated a distance of 240 kilometers ($4 \times 50 = 200$ in the first four days, and $4 \times 10 = 40$ in the second four days).

A WORD ABOUT SPACING BETWEEN ARMORED VEHICLES

The potential of area weapons such as SFW to service columns of armored vehicles (measured in kilometers) *is strictly independent of the spacing between those armored vehicles.* If the unimpeded advance is 70 kilometers per day and firepower can attack 50 kilometers of armored columns per day at DE > 0.7, the net advance of unattacked vehicles is 20 kilometers per day regardless of spacing.

If one were attacking with area munitions only, spacing would affect both how *long* the attack must be sustained and how *many* armored vehicles are damaged per day. For example, doubling the spacing doubles the time required—by halving the rate at which vehicles can enter the line of advance—and halves the kills per day. Given sufficient weapons, over the length of an entire campaign the total number of armored vehicles damaged will not be changed significantly by spacing, because the changes in duration and kills per day tend to cancel each other.

With one-on-one weapons like Maverick, however, spacing affects duration *but not weapon effectiveness.* In other words, doubling the spacing still doubles the load time—the period of time required to load a given number of armored vehicles onto a path of advance. But there is no impact on the damage expectancy from one-on-one weapons (i.e., the effectiveness is not halved as with area munitions). Thus, if the enemy increases the spacing, one-on-one kills in a given time period are unchanged but the length of time the enemy is vulnerable is doubled.

The discussion above suggests that, given a particular spacing between armored vehicles, one could find an optimal mix of area munitions and one-on-one weapons that enforce a floor on firepower's halt capacity—i.e., whereby the capacity could be no lower. In other words, if the enemy increased his spacing to reduce the effectiveness of area munitions, this would slow his rate of advance. Because of the presence of one-on-one weapons, however, *there would not be a commensurate reduction in the number of armored vehicles damaged.* On the other hand, if he reduced his spacing to accelerate the arrival of a given number of vehicles to a certain penetration distance, the effectiveness of the area munitions would rise, thereby increasing the number of vehicles damaged. Thus, increasing or reducing the spacing in relation to the optimum benefits only the defender.

BASELINE INPUTS AND OUTCOME MEASURES

Individual platform characteristics are shown in Table A.2. These include weapons loads, sortie rates used in our base case, and degrade factors affecting sortie effectiveness and weapon use.

The spreadsheet methods used for this analysis generate a number of output measures of interest to the analyst. For each day, the spreadsheet details the distance advanced by unattacked enemy units, the total number of vehicles destroyed and reaching their objective, vehicles destroyed by platform type, and weapons expended by type.

Table A.2
Platform Characteristics

Platform	Area Weapon		1 v 1 Weapon			1 v 1 SSPK	Sortie Rate	Sortie Degrade	% Weapon Return
	WCMD Load	JSOW Load	ATACMS Load	Hellfire Load	Maverick Load				
B-1	30	0	0	0	0	0.00	0.75	0.57	0.50
F-15 E	8	0	0	0	2	0.50	1.67	0.57	0.50
F-16	4	0	0	0	2	0.50	2.00	0.57	0.50
F-18 E	0	4	0	0	2	0.50	2.00	0.57	0.50
A-10	0	0	0	0	4	0.50	2.00	0.57	0.50
ATACMS	0	0	1	0	0	4.00	1.00	0.57	0.00
Helos	0	0	0	8	0	0.50	2.00	0.57	0.50

Weapon loadouts: To ensure consistency in the weapons limit calculations, platforms are assumed to carry one type of area weapon and/or one type of 1 v 1 weapon. Area weapons (WCMD and JSOW in this analysis) are preferred and are used until stocks are depleted. In this construct, ATACMS, helicopters, and A-10s carrying guided missiles are treated as direct attack or "1 v 1" weapons. This makes some sense, because helicopters and A-10s are clearly 1 v 1 platforms and ATACMS/BAT kills are largely insensitive to the vehicle spacing calculations applied to WCMD/JSOW. In practical terms, this means that use of these platforms does not decrement available WCMD and JSOW stocks.

1 v 1 SSPK is the single-sortie/shot probability of kill for each 1 v 1 weapon carried by the platform. Note that this value is greater than 1.0 for the case of ATACMS.

Sortie rate is the number of sorties per day available from each platform. In the case of the ATACMS, each missile shot is counted as one "sortie." For enhanced survivability, attack helicopters are assumed to fly only at night during the halt phase.

Sortie degrade is the fraction of sorties that engage a valid target. Other sorties are assumed to be "wasted" for various reasons—failure to find valid targets, aborts, or attacks against non-armored vehicles. We degrade sorties by more than one-third.

% Weapon return is the fraction of unsuccessful sorties that return with their weapons. This is used to calculate weapons expenditures. Here it is assumed that for all weapons except ATACMS one half of the sorties that do not engage a valid target return to base with their ordnance.